The VEGETARIAN MANIFESTO

By Cheryl L. Perry, Leslie A. Lytle and Teresa G. Jacobs

RUNNING PRESS

PHILADELPHIA · LONDON

9 8 7 6 5 4 3 2 1

Digit on the right indicates the number of this printing

Library of Congress Control Number: 2004090638

ISBN 0-7624-1887-7

Cover illustration by Gina Triplett

Cover and interior design by Dustin Summers

Edited by Jennifer Kasius

Typography: Akzidenze Grotesk

This book may be ordered by mail from the publisher. Please include $2.50 for postage and handling.
But try your bookstore first!

Running Press Book Publishers

125 South Twenty-second Street

Philadelphia, Pennsylvania 19103-4399

Visit us on the web!

www.runningpress.com

contents

introduction

IF YOU'RE A YOUNG PERSON WHO HAS BECOME OR IS THINKING ABOUT BECOMING A VEGETARIAN, CONGRATULATIONS! YOU HAVE MADE—OR ARE ABOUT TO MAKE—WHAT MIGHT BE THE MOST IMPORTANT DECISION IN YOUR LIFE—A DECISION TO IMPROVE YOUR HEALTH, MAINTAIN THE PLANET, AND PROTECT ANIMALS THAT ARE KILLED UNNECESSARILY EVERY DAY.

Vegetarianism among teenagers in America is on the rise, but it is still very much in the minority. Overall, about 6 percent of teens at any one time are vegetarians. Among high school students, 14 percent—close to one in seven teens—have been vegetarians at some time in their young lives. So if you've made the switch, consider yourself part of an elite group!

But are you curious about what other teen vegetarians eat, why they become vegetarian, what being vegetarian means to them, and how their family and friends react to the news? Do you wonder what advice others might give you? If you answered "yes" to any of these questions, then this book is meant for you!

There are dozens of books on vegetarianism, particularly loads of cookbooks with recipes for all kinds of vegetarian snacks and meals. There are also plenty of guides on vegetarian nutrition that provide information on what to eat to be at your healthiest. No book, however, has been written from your perspective—from one vegetarian teen to another—until now.

The three of us are currently at the University of Minnesota. Two of us

(Cheryl Perry and Leslie Lytle) are professors and Teresa Jacobs is a recent graduate of the School of Public Health. Cheryl and Leslie have conducted surveys with teens concerning alcohol, drugs, eating, physical activity, and vegetarianism for the past 20 years. Leslie is also a registered dietitian, while Teresa has specialized in teen vegetarism. As a group, we decided that the survey research we had been doing just wasn't able to tell the *whole* story of the *real* experiences of teen vegetarians. We also felt that direct advice from teens was important for those who wanted to become vegetarian, so we decided to do this book in a different way. We conducted group discussions with young vegetarians, one-on-one interviews, while also posting questions on various teen vegetarian websites to obtain your perspectives for this book. Thus, most of the book includes quotes from teens on their personal experiences and stories. We have also tried to provide some guidance throughout the book whenever issues were raised that we felt needed clarifying. Our interviews and research show that there's a wealth of knowledge, opinions, and experiences to be shared—which is all compiled in this book.

Over the course of our research, we found that vegetarians were more likely than nonvegetarians to be eating healthfully, but we also determined that younger vegetarians were susceptible to weight-related eating problems. Much of what we discovered in our research is reported in this book. But instead of us telling the story, the story will be told by teens and young adults. You hear about concerns and advice in their own words. To protect their identities, we do not give out their names, ages, or hometowns. But we *can* tell you that they are teens just like you, from all over the United States.

Because you had so much to say on the topic, we feel this book is a true "manifesto" of your feelings, ideals, values, and ideas. You can read the book in any order you'd like, by the topics of most interest to you. We hope that you feel like you, the reader, are also having a conversation with your peers!

Cheryl L. Perry, MA, PhD, Professor, Division of Epidemiology, School of Public Health, University of Minnesota

Leslie A. Lytle, RD, PhD, Professor, Division of Epidemiology, School of Public Health, University of Minnesota

Teresa G. Jacobs, MPH, Division of Epidemiology, School of Public Health, University of Minnesota

a choice worth making

DESPITE ALL THE KNOWN HEALTH AND ENVIRONMENTAL BENEFITS OF A PLANT-BASED DIET, THE UNITED STATES IS STILL VERY MUCH A MEAT-BASED NATION. THIS MEANS THAT YOU ARE TURNING TO VEGETARIANISM FOR REASONS THAT HAVE NOTHING TO DO WITH "FITTING IN." YOU ARE DOING IT BECAUSE:

- You believe that animals are being mistreated, especially with current slaughtering methods for meat.

- You realize that more people can be fed on a plant-based vegetarian diet and believe this is needed as the population of the world increases.

- You know that vegetarianism has definite health benefits.

- You've discovered the environmental benefits to farming crops rather than clearing land for animals.

- You know that humans can survive very well nutritionally without eating any meat.

Most likely one, or maybe all, of these reasons describes where you are in your life today!

Vegetarianism: What Is It?

This is a question you are likely to hear over and over again.

Vegetarianism is not a "diet." Yes, it means cutting out certain foods—animal-based products, mostly meat—and adding plant-based products, such as soy. But vegetarianism is really a lifestyle that involves eating and using as few animal products as possible, while still maintaining personal health and well-being. Changing to a plant-based diet is a courageous act. You are making the decision not to eat like "everyone else" but to eat in a way that is more healthful and respectful to yourself and the environment around you.

The Benefits

We want you to feel good and be as healthy as possible. The good news is that there are many personal benefits to a vegetarian lifestyle. The first is the knowledge that you are not harming another living creature when it is unnecessary to do so. Many vegetarians feel better about themselves for making the decision not to harm animals.

The second is that being vegetarian is good for your heart and cardiovascular system. Vegetarians are much less likely to have heart disease than nonvegetarians.

The third is that vegetarians are less likely to become obese as adults—and obesity is definitely a rising problem in the United States. It's also a problem with lots of health consequences, such as diabetes and cancer.

Fourth, vegetarians, on average, live longer than nonvegetarians. So this decision has consequences that are very positive, especially for those who are vegetarian throughout most of their lives.

Potential Pitfalls

But there are some things to watch out for when you give up meat. Teens, in general, do not get enough calcium, and vegetarians run the risk of getting even less. Calcium is a mineral essential to the bone development that is still taking place during teenage growth. If bones don't develop properly, this can lead later in life to the brittle-bone disease known as osteoporosis.

It may be that you view vegetarianism as a weight-loss tactic and therefore fail to replace the meat you are giving up with other nonmeat proteins, such as soy, milk products, wheat gluten, legumes, and nuts. Bear in mind that those who view vegetarianism as a weight-loss diet are also more likely to try other kinds of unhealthy eating patterns, such as binge eating and purging.

Remember that vegetarianism, in itself, will not necessarily cause you to lose weight. But the vegetarian lifestyle of eating healthfully and doing other health-promoting activities like walking or bicycling (good for the environment!) should all add up to keep you at a healthy weight.

A Positive Approach

This book will help you to become a healthy vegetarian. You'll be learning from others your age how they do it, what is easy, and what might be a challenge. Each of you is different. That is why we spoke to a diverse group that had one thing in common: support of the vegetarian life. Throughout this book, you should find many in situations that you can relate to on a variety of topics. Hopefully, they will help you solve your problems, answer your questions, and alleviate your concerns.

We believe that every person who becomes a vegetarian helps make the world a better place, so we want you to succeed!

vegetarianism:

WHAT IT MEANS

NOW THAT YOU'RE VEGETARIAN, IT IS LIKELY YOU'LL BE GRILLED BY YOUR FRIENDS AND ADULTS (ESPECIALLY YOUR PARENTS) ABOUT YOUR NEW LIFESTYLE. YOU MAY BE ASKED: *WHAT IS A VEGETARIAN? WHAT DOES IT MEAN TO BE A "VEG" OR "VEGAN"?* YOU MAY EVEN BE WONDERING WHAT KIND OF VEGETARIAN YOU WANT TO BE, AND WHAT IT ALL MEANS.

Deep Feelings

Question: *What is the one word you would use to describe a vegetarian?*

Replies:

"Compassionate. Vegs feel reverence for all beings. Animals have feelings, too."

"Smart. We are the future. It's smart to choose a diet that keeps us, and our planet, healthy."

"Different. Although there are a lot more veggie eaters now than when I first started, we are still different from the majority!"

"Healthy. It becomes a lifestyle. You're vegetarian, eventually, maybe after a few years, you move towards veganism. The longer you do it, the healthier you feel and the more you love it."

"Maybe compassionate. (But I know all vegans aren't exactly compassionate.) Or dedicated, aware, or empathetic, too. Animals are being mistreated, the environment is being abused, and people are getting fatter. Now that I'm aware of these problems, I do my share in the solution by choosing vegetarianism."

"Radical. Because our society embraces a 'bigger is better' philosophy and is willing to use any resource available, including animals, for economic gain, it's radical to choose vegetarianism. Vegs, in essence, ask society to slow down, take a step back, and look at the harm they're causing."

Teen Terms

We discovered in our research that *vegetarianism* suggests a variety of eating patterns. For example, nearly half of the vegetarian teens who shared their views with us say that they eat chicken and fish. To others, being a vegetarian means going strictly animal-free.

Question: *What kind of vegetarian are you?*

Replies:

"I'm just a general vegetarian. I don't eat meat or fish, and dairy products make me sick. Sometimes I feel like people get mad at me when they have to prepare something different because I'm a vegetarian. Maybe I make them feel guilty for eating meat. Sometimes I call eggs 'fetus' or 'embryo' because I want people to be aware of what it really is they are eating. By setting an example, I might influence others to choose vegetarianism."

There's certainly diversity among vegetarians. Almost all avoid eating meat, though some will eat fish and others will consume fish and chicken. Then there are those who avoid milk, fish, animal by-products or anything that is cooked. It all comes down to personal choice. If you want to put yourself in a category, check out the following descriptions of the different types of vegetarians.

lacto-ovo vegetarian: Avoids eating the flesh of animals but will eat eggs (ovo) and dairy (lacto) products. A lacto-vegetarian will eat dairy products but not eggs and an ovo-vegetarian will eat eggs but not dairy.

vegan: Avoids consuming all foods of animal origin, including eggs, dairy, gelatin and honey. Also refrains from wearing animal products, such as leather shoes or wool and silk clothes.

raw foodist: Eats a largely uncooked diet, or a completely uncooked diet. Such diets consist of fruits, vegetables, sprouts, nuts, seeds, dried fruit, and fresh juices.

pesco-vegetarian: Will eat fish but avoids eating other animal flesh.

pollo-vegetarian: Will eat chicken but not other animal flesh.

semi-vegetarian: Mostly avoids eating meat, chicken, and fish but will eat them occasionally.

freegan: A vegan consumer who will eat food containing eggs or dairy, but only when it is free of cost and would otherwise be wasted.

fruitarian: Eats only the fruits from plants, grains, nuts, seeds, legumes, tomatoes and eggplant.

sproutarian: Eats primarily sprouted seeds such as bean, wheat or broccoli sprouts, usually supplemented with other raw foods.

macrobiotic: Eats locally-grown whole foods such as grains, fresh vegetables, sea vegetables and beans, and may eat small amounts of white fish. A person who follows a macrobiotic diet often follows a religious philosophy emphasizing a simple life in harmony with nature.

"My father currently is a vegan. He's been vegan since my parents' divorce, when he started living alone. I don't think I could avoid all animal products like he does (he won't even eat bread or gelatin!). I really love milk and other dairy products, so I'd really miss those foods. Meat, on the other hand, I can and do live without. If I come to a point in my life when veganism feels like the right thing for me, I'll give it a try. But I'm not ready yet."

gelatin, no; bread, yes

Gelatin is a vegetarian issue because it is made by boiling the tissues—skin, ligaments and bones—of slaughtered animals. As a result, most strict vegetarians shun foods made with it, such as Jell-O, marshmallows, jams, jellies and some candies.

Most breads, on the other hand, contain no animal products. The exception is specialty breads made with egg or cheese. If you are a lacto-ovo, most any bread will do!

"I'm a fairly strict vegan. I've been through stricter periods, when I never ate anything if I didn't know exactly what was in it and where it came from, but now I'm more open to compromise. My life is easier this way; I can enjoy food more without worrying about every little detail. When I first became vegan I didn't know anything about nutrition. I didn't even know much about preparing food, because no one in my family cooks. It took a while, but now I have a wide exposure to all sorts of different foods and have an interest in other new things.

But with hygiene products I try really hard to buy things that are organic and vegan. I suppose that if I was on a road trip or something, I might buy something that was just sort of normal."

"I'm a vegan and I think veganism is pretty adaptable most of the time. Some people say that veganism means no animal products—ever. The way I understand it, veganism means 'use as few animal products as you can' to lead to a life that's happy and fulfilling and meaningful. I don't like rigid boundaries."

check your hygiene products

If you want to avoid animal products entirely, then you should check out your bathroom cabinet. Many hygiene and personal care products use ingredients that come from animals, such as gelatin. So check labels. If you want to avoid hygiene products that use animal products, check out Tom's of Maine, a family-owned company based in Kennebunk, Maine (http://www.tomsofmaine.com).

"I'm a vegan *unless* the eggs come from free-range chickens and the milk is free of bovine growth hormones. In that case, I'm a lacto-ovo vegetarian."

"I try to avoid anything that comes from an animal: meat, dairy, eggs, honey, and other animal by-products like gelatin and whey. I choose vegan clothes; you won't find any leather, fur, or silk in my wardrobe. Unfortunately, I don't pay attention to what's in my cosmetics, or whether the company tests on animals. I think it's hard to be completely vegan in this society. I do the best I can to live without causing harm to the world around me."

what are they putting in our milk?

The milk you drink may include hormones and antibiotics.

Some cows are given a hormone called "bovine somatotropin" (BST) or "recombinant bovine growth hormone" (rBGH) in order to increase their milk production. These hormones have been approved by the USA's Food and Drug Administration with evidence that they are safe for human consumption. Authorities in other countries are not so sure, however, and have restricted their use in the dairy industry. If you want to drink milk that is free from BST and rBGH, look on the label to see if your milk is "hormone-free."

Farmers may also use antibiotics to prevent the spread of infection in herds, so your milk may contain traces of antibiotics in them. Some folks fear that the antibiotics given to animals raised for food production will lead to an increase in antibiotic-resistant microorganisms in the human body, meaning antibiotics taken to fight infection will become less effective over time.

"I decided I was going to become vegetarian one day and then I slowly dropped meat. I still eat eggs, milk, and sometimes fish. I usually just have textured vegetable protein, which is like fake meat. You can use it in tacos or sloppy joes. And I eat a lot of tofu."

tvp—the best tacos ever!

TVP gets its acronym from its official name, Textured Vegetable Protein. Also known as TSP (Textured Soy Protein), it is made from soy flour that has had the oil removed. It comes in a variety of forms—flakes, chunks, granules—that are rehydrated with water and then used as a substitute for ground meat. It is high in protein, absorbs flavors, and makes a great base for tacos, tostados, and sloppy joes.

household cleaners

Most household cleaners are made with products derived from animals. Many are also tested on animals, which goes against the philosophy of strict vegetarians.

Vegetarians opposed to such products have turned to natural cleaners because they also help reduce the impact of toxic chemicals on the environment. Products like pure soap flakes, borax, essential oils, and vinegar can be found in local hardware and natural food grocery stores, and can be used in different ways to make gentle and effective household cleaners.

If you are not sure whether a product used in your household is derived from an animal, check out the website www.peta.org/mall/cc/ingred.html. Another good resource is "Animal Ingredients and Their Alternatives" on the website www.caring-consumer.com/ingredientsfactsheet.html.

Making Choices

Now you can see that there are many types of vegetarians—from those who avoid all animal products to those who occasionally eat fish and chicken. We wanted to find out how teens began the process of becoming vegetarian.

Question: *When you decided to become vegetarian, what changes did you make to your diet?*

Replies:

"Before I became vegetarian I based my meals on the Food Guide Pyramid. I shifted the pyramid a little, though, to make it heavier on the whole grains and vegetables. I cut out a whole lot of fatty foods by doing that."

"I started making myself protein shakes with fruit, yogurt, and granola. As meat substitutes, my dad started buying me veggie burgers and textured vegetable protein. And (of course!) now that I'm vegetarian, I eat a lot of salads. Salads are great, too, because restaurants always offer them."

"First, I cut out the meat from my diet but didn't replace it with anything. And then I started losing a lot of weight and my mom was scared, so she started buying vegetarian products like tofu and soy beans. Later I stopped eating fish, and now I'm drinking a lot of milk and eating a lot of cheese."

"[My parents] got me a nutritionist. It was just for starting out, making sure I did it right. She showed me how to make tofu taste good, by marinating it or putting it into soups. She also introduced me to a lot of other cool, new foods. She proved that a vegetarian diet is anything but boring! It can (and should) include so much more than salad."

how to find a nutritionist

While it is pretty easy to eat a nutritious diet if you are a lacto- or ovo-vegetarian, a strict vegan diet may bring more challenges—especially getting enough protein, calcium, zinc, iron, and vitamin B_{12}. Some great resources on how to eat a healthful vegan diet are:

- *Becoming Vegan* by Vesonto Melina and Brenda Davis
- The Vegetarian Resource Group: www.vrg.org
- The Vegetarian Practice Group of the American Dietetic Association: www.Andrews.edu/NUFS/vndpg.html.

If you want to talk to someone about planning a healthful vegan diet, look in the phone book in your town for a Registered Dietitian or call the Dietetics department of your local hospital or clinic and ask for a referral to a Registered Dietitian.

"I started eating a few small meals a day, instead of two or three big ones. I used to hate the feeling of having eaten too much meat. My stomach is much happier filled with veggies, whole grains, and fruit."

quinoa: king of the grains

Quinoa (pronounced KEEN-wah) is the "supergrain" that has more high-quality protein than any other grain. Quinoa is a small seed that in size, shape, and color looks like a cross between sesame seed and millet.

The high mountainous regions of Ecuador, Peru, Bolivia, southern Colombia, and northern Argentina and Chile grow most of the world's quinoa.

Cook quinoa in water and use it like you would rice or couscous. For example, you can top it with stir-fried vegetables or use it in a cold grain salad.

"When I first started off as a vegetarian, I was very unhealthy. Instead of eating chicken, I had a candy bar or some other kind of junk food. After six months of that, I decided to use the internet to find out what vegetarians are supposed to eat to get their protein. Now that I'm better informed and therefore choosing healthy meat alternatives, my skin is clear, my hair is shiny, and my nails are strong. That's how I identify healthiness."

"I eat soy and dairy so I have enough protein and I take more vitamins (calcium) than I did before."

"We eat a lot of tortillas. You can make them into pizzas with tomato sauce and cheese, or burritos with rice, beans, and salsa."

"I make vegetarian burgers. I've made the chicken type too, but it's veggie chicken."

"We eat a lot of pasta: spaghetti sauce without the meat, or noodles and butter."

"I stopped eating meat and instead ate whatever in the meal wasn't meat. My family wasn't very supportive, so they didn't cook me meals. In stir-fries, for example, I ate the vegetables instead of the chicken. When I became vegan, I wasn't very educated about vegan foods, so I ate peanut butter sandwiches for a few weeks. And then I read some cookbooks and found out about things like quinoa and all these crazy vegetables and started incorporating them into my diet."

"I became a more responsible consumer. I buy cruelty-free. I don't wear leather, fur, or wool. I am more environmentally concerned. I am basically the whole vegan package. When I say I am vegan, it means that I avoid all animal products."

"When I became vegan, I didn't know what I was doing. I filled up on bread until I learned that you have to replace meat and dairy products with other sources of protein, vitamins, and minerals. Now I try to have a protein source in all of my meals. I eat more nuts and beans. I eat tofu, too, even though I used to think it was absolutely disgusting."

Protein Sources for Vegetarians

PROTEIN SOURCE	WHAT IS IT?	HOW DO YOU USE IT?
Textured Vegetable Protein (TVP) or Textured Soy Protein (TSP)	Soy flour with the oil removed. It comes dry in granules, flakes, and chunks.	Add water and use it as a ground-meat substitute in foods like chili, tacos, or sloppy joes.
Seitan (SAY-tan)	Wheat gluten (from flour) kneaded with water, rolled into a roast shape, and boiled.	Seitan comes in a variety of forms and can be sliced and eaten like a beef roast, used in stews in place of meat, or eaten as a seitan "burger".
Tempeh (tem-PAY)	A flat cake made from fermented soybeans.	Grill it, sauté it, and eat it in sandwiches, or use it in casserole.
Tofu	"Cheese" made from soy milk. It can be hard or soft and has little taste on its own.	Best used with other foods, such as stir-fries and in pasta dishes, or blended with fruits or other flavorings for a dairylike dessert.
Tahini	A paste made from ground sesame seeds.	Use on sandwiches or in dips and sauces.
Nut butters (peanut, soy, almond)	Pureed nuts.	Use as a spread on sandwiches or crackers.
Edamame (ay-da-MOM-ee)	Sweet-tasting, large-seeded soybeans.	Serve cooked as a side dish or add to rice dishes, casseroles, soups, salad, or stir-fries.

Meat, Ick!

Question: *How do you avoid meat in meals? For example, if you were served a stew containing meat, would you eat around the meat or not eat the stew at all?*

Replies:

"I'm not that picky. For example, it doesn't bother me when a vegetable soup is made with beef broth. As a vegetarian, there is enough for me to watch out for without analyzing everything to death."

"I don't eat anything with meat. I don't even pick the meat out, because the residue is too gross. Problems arise, though, when I have to tell someone I won't eat what they've cooked. I can't just say it's too gross. And when I explain that I'm a vegetarian, they tell me to pick the meat out. It's rude to pick out the meat and too much work. I'd rather make myself something simple, like pasta and tomato sauce, or a big salad with garbanzo beans.

"For the first year that I was vegetarian, I picked the meat out of everything. Then I realized that chicken broth is chicken-flavored because the bird was cooked in it, and other meats, like bacon, add flavor to the entire dish. I decided that I don't want to eat anything that an animal died for, even if that means making myself a separate meal."

A Wearness Issue

Question: What other kinds of changes have you made?

Replies:

"I pay more attention to other ways we use animals. I don't buy leather shoes, and I don't like to see people wearing fur."

"Being vegan or vegetarian has even made me think about where everything I use comes from and where it's going. I don't shop at new clothing stores anymore, because I know too much about bad labor conditions. And I don't use Styrofoam, because it does not easily decompose and is toxic when burned. I learn as much as I can about what the materials are and then make choices that will have the least impact on the planet."

"I switched to vegan toothpaste and vegan soap. I can't find any vegan deodorant, so I don't use it. It's kind of a problem sometimes!"

a good vegan deodorant

A vegetarian deodorant means it has not been tested on animals and does not contain artificial preservatives, flavors, colors, sweeteners, or animal ingredients.

Tom's of Maine (www.tomsofmaine.com), for example, makes a variety of deodorants that are vegan, including Honeysuckle Rose and Gentle Woodspice.

Many people who get rashes from traditional deodorants find that vegan deodorants are easier on sensitive skin and smell great.

Sheep's Clothing

The subject of wool as a vegetarian taboo creates lively dialogue, even though wool comes from shearing sheep, not killing them. Concern, if any, comes from the possibility that a sheep will be injured during the shearing process or mistreated during confinement.

Question: *What do you think about wearing wool clothing?*

Replies:

"I agree with not eating animal products and not wearing leather, but wool? Surely shearing sheep doesn't hurt them very badly—just little knicks and scratches. Isn't it better for the wool to come off, anyway?"

"I wear wool, mostly because it's practical for Canadian winters. I know there are other warm fabrics, but wool is warmer and more affordable than most of them."

"In the shearing process, many of the sheep get cut with the clippers, often quite badly. They also are corralled and manhandled. Many vegans disagree with corralling animals because the conditions in corals can be crowded and unsanitary (this is bound to make the sheep unhappy)."

"Wool is like eggs or milk, in a way. Sure, for a while the purpose of the animal is production, but sooner or later they wind up at the meat packer."

Beyond Meat

There are discussions on websites about foods that vegetarians feel may or may not be appropriate to eat.

Question: *What foods should or shouldn't vegetarians eat? What about sugar, honey, or other refined carbohydrates?*

Posting:

"Is it possible to eat too much fruit? The food pyramid says that you need 2–3 servings a day. Since I became a vegetarian, I eat much more than that!"

Replies:

"You will hear plenty about people who are raw foodists [and] eat only fruits and veggies. Some say you have more energy and better skin.

So if five a day is good, is eating fifty a day even better?

We believe that a plant-based diet is very healthy, but you can eat too much of a good thing. Overall, there is no problem with eating a lot of fruits and veggies, however, too much can may cause an upset stomach, or diarrhea. Also, if you eat too many fruits and veggies you may miss out on other important food groups such as whole grains and protein sources.

Don't forget that fruits and veggies **do** contain calories. Eating anything in excess can lead to eating more calories than you need and result in unhealthy weight gain.

Also, remember to wash your fruits and veggies well to wash off any pesticides. Better yet, buy organic.

I am partially raw right now and considering going totally raw! Refined sugar is refined with pork bones, so most of us vegans don't eat it."

"Beyond the bone char concerns and health-related issues, there are many factors to consider when purchasing sugar and products that contain it. The vast majority of sugar cane is not organically grown, and most sugar plantations employ environmentally unsound agricultural methods, such as heavy insecticide and pesticide use and crop burning."

the scoop on sugar

The rumor that sugar is taboo for vegetarians has been going around for decades. At one time it was an issue but it isn't anymore.

Before the 1950s cane sugar was sometimes whitened using animal bones. Now the sugar industry uses charcoal-type sources from plants. If you want to avoid cane sugar, choose sugar made from sugar beets or organic sugar, or substitute ⅔ to 1 cup dried cane-juice granules for each cup of white sugar. For more information, check out www.wholesomesweetners.com.

Posting: *Many people are interested in why vegans don't eat honey. What do you say when people ask you that?*

Reply:

"I explain to them that there are five or six different reasons. For instance, the queen bee's wings are clipped, so she can't fly away. And the bees are fed sugar to shorten their lives and make a sweeter honey. Nobody cares about killing thousands of bees when they're changing the combs. Also, they are ruining the diversity of the species of bees by overproducing one species. Many people understand this mistreatment is taking place, but they eat honey anyway."

the big deal with honey

Many vegans choose not to eat honey because they believe that the practice of bee keeping is enslavement, and therefore inhumane.

Honey is produced by honeybees and collected from the hive by beekeepers. In addition to producing honey, the bees that are managed by keepers are also rented out to farmers to help pollinate crops.

Practices such as hive burning, the use of antibiotics to protect bees against parasites, and agricultural use of pesticides on crops are all cited as reasons that people should not eat honey.

If you are opposed to this practice, you can substitute 1 cup of barley malt syrup or rice syrup for every $\frac{3}{4}$ cup of honey.

Posting: What about eating potatoes?

Replies:

"Potatoes are empty calories. If you aren't trying to lose weight, then go for it; just don't have a potato-based diet (I'm sure you don't). Fruit juices are often empty calories, too. They are made from mostly sugar and artificial colors and flavors."

"Potatoes are a quality, whole complex carbohydrate, and they always make me feel good. Of course, I won't eat them if they're made into deep-fried French fries, but they're hardly potatoes at that point."

fruit juice: not sugar in disguise

One hundred percent fruit juice—that is, juice that is not sweetened, fruit-flavored water—is a great source of nutrients. There is natural sugar in fruit juice, just as there is natural sugar in whole fruit (natural fruit sugar is called *fructose*), and both fruit juice and fruits can be great choices in a vegetarian or vegan diet.

Here's the one thing to watch out for, though: It is easy to drink a lot of juice, and with that juice comes lots of calories. Whole fruit is more satisfying because it takes longer to eat and is often more filling because it contains more fiber. By eating fruit rather than its juice, you will be satisfied on less. Here is an example:

1 cup of orange juice = 110 calories, 2 grams of protein, 82 mg of vitamin C, and 0 grams of fiber.

1 whole orange = 62 calories, 1 gram of protein, 70 mg of vitamin C, and 3 grams of fiber.

potatoes: thumbs up

Yes, potatoes can be part of a healthy vegetarian diet. Eating a baked potato with the skin gives you 5 grams of protein, 5 grams of fiber, nearly 3 milligrams of iron, and zero fat!

Potatoes do contain a lot of carbohydrate (55 grams in a baked potato with skin) but it is complex carbohydrate, with more fiber than refined carbohydrates. A diet rich in complex carbohydrates has many health benefits, including a lowered risk of obesity, adult-onset (Type 2) diabetes, and some cancers.

Try microwaving white or sweet potatoes (pierce them with a fork and microwave on high for 8 to 10 minutes) and top them with stir-fried veggies or beans for a quick and nutritious meal.

"Potatoes are good and wholesome foods that provide quality complex carbohydrates, in addition to some other micronutrients. Many people have become convinced (by diet gurus like Atkins) that potatoes make people fat, etc., whereas the reality is the opposite. If people ate more vegetables, they wouldn't get so fat in the first place."

Posting: *And what about refined flour? Should vegetarians eat it?*

Reply:

"I got rid of all the enriched flour/bleached flour in my diet, but now I feel like I am eating nothing. I eat tons of fruit and veggies, and a pita or two a day with hummus or almond butter. I eat a lot of granola and beans, too, but I still never feel full."

Response to reply:

"You can't remain full on fruit and veggies alone. Getting rid of refined flour is good, but you need to replace it with whole-grain products. I can suggest whole-wheat pasta, brown rice, corn/whole-wheat/spelt tortillas, whole-grain breads, sprouted bread or bagels, barley, quinoa etc. There are tons of unrefined grains out there. Try to eat a variety of different grains so that you will get all your essential vitamins and minerals."

Get Information, Not Misinformation

Given the depth of knowledge these teens revealed about vegan foods, we wondered how they were getting their information.

Question: *Is there a good vegan food guide that you follow?*

Replies:

" Vesanto Melina and Brenda Davis, two vegetarian registered dietitians who authored *Becoming Vegan*, recommend the following for vegans:

- 6–11 servings per day of whole grains (bread, cereal, whole grains, pasta).

- 3 or more servings per day of vegetables (a wide variety of colorful vegetables; bright colors indicate the presence of antioxidants; green vegetables are rich sources of folate).

- 2 or more servings of fruit.

- 2–3 servings of beans and bean alternatives (beans, tofu, nuts, seeds, tempeh, "veggie meats").

- 6–8 servings calcium-fortified soy milk and calcium alternates.

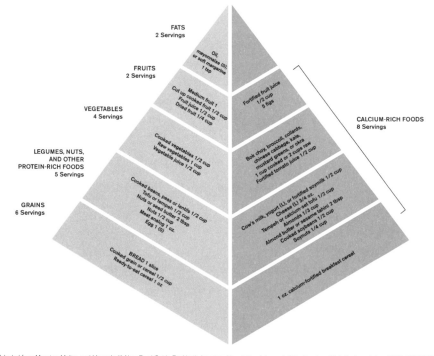

FATS
2 Servings

FRUITS
2 Servings

VEGETABLES
4 Servings

LEGUMES, NUTS, AND OTHER PROTEIN-RICH FOODS
5 Servings

GRAINS
6 Servings

CALCIUM-RICH FOODS
8 Servings

Oil, mayonnaise (O), or soft margarine 1 tsp

Medium fruit 1
Cut up cooked fruit 1/2 cup
Fruit Juice 1/2 cup
Dried fruit 1/4 cup

Fortified fruit juice 1/2 cup
5 figs

Cooked vegetables 1/2 cup
Raw vegetables 1 cup
Vegetable juice 1/2 cup

Bok choy, broccoli, collards, chinese cabbage, kale, mustard greens, or okra 1 cup cooked or 2 cups raw
Fortified tomato juice 1/2 cup

Cooked beans, peas or lentils 1/2 cup
Tofu or tempeh 1/2 cup
Nuts or seed butter 2 tbsp
Meat analog 1 oz.
Egg 1 (O)

Cow's milk, yogurt (L), or fortified soymilk 1/2 cup
Cheese (L) 3/4 oz.
Tempeh or calcium-set tofu 1/2 cup
Almonds 1/3 cup
Almond butter or sesame tahini 2 tbsp
Cooked soybeans 1/4 cup
Soynuts 1/4 cup

Cooked grain or cereal 1/2 cup
BREAD 1 slice
Ready-to-eat cereal 1 oz

1 oz. calcium-fortified breakfast cereal

Adapted from Messina, Melina, and Mangels, "A New Food Guide For North American Vegetarians," Journal of the American Dietetic Association; 2003, 103 (6):771-775
All items are vegan unless noted as ovo (O) with eggs or lacto (L) with milk

- 1–2 servings omega-3 fatty acids (1 teaspoon flaxseed oil or 1 tablespoon ground flaxseeds constitutes a serving; canola oil, soy foods, and walnuts also have some omega-3s).

- Vitamin B_{12}, either in a supplement supplying about 2.5 micrograms a day (or take a 25 microgram tablet every week—the body can store it), or B_{12} in fortified foods such as cereals and Red Star Vegetarian Support Formula nutritional yeast flakes.

- Vitamin D—if you don't get at least 15 minutes of sunshine on the bare skin of your arms and face, you need 10–15 micrograms a day of vitamin D.

They also recommend that you be moderate in your intake of saturated fats, oils, and sugars, get at least 30 minutes of physical activity per day, and drink 6 to 8 glasses of water daily."

Summing it Up

- Vegetarians come in many varieties—vegans, fregans, ovo-lacto, lacto-, pollo- and pesco- vegetarians. Most of you agree, though, that those who eat chicken, fish, and meat are not "true" vegetarians.

- Many of you are concerned about animals and how they have been treated for the purpose of slaughtering for human consumption. As a result, the strictest vegetarians also avoid animal by-products, such as gelatin and honey.

- Soy products such as veggie burgers and tofu are widely eaten to replace meat.

- There are vegan and vegetarian food-guide pyramids to help you choose what to eat.

the vegetarian attitude

VEGETARIANISM IS CLEARLY NOT THE NORM IN OUR SOCIE-
TY. THAT MEANS THAT YOU ARE STEPPING OUT ON A LIMB,
SO TO SPEAK, WHEN YOU SWITCH TO A VEGETARIAN DIET—AND A
VEGETARIAN LIFESTYLE.

It is considered a lifestyle because it is emotions, not eating preferences, that usually drive the decision to convert. Emotions that stem from regard for the environment, compassion for the welfare of animals that are slaughtered for human consumption, interest in personal health, and concern for the future of planet Earth. It takes courage to do something so different!

Beyond this, there are specific and personal reasons and often a particular event that help motivate the change. What is it that drove you to this lifestyle? What motivates you to stick with it? We sense that these beliefs must be very strong and provocative to lead to such a drastic change in diet.

So we asked you why you became vegetarian and probed environmental concerns, animal rights, personal health, spiritual health, and weight management as potential reasons. We also wanted to find out what personal benefits being a vegetarian had already provided. Was the decision to be a vegetarian rewarded in some ways even in the first few weeks?

Generally, vegetarians lead cleaner lives because concern for personal health is a big motivator. So we asked what other lifestyle issues went along with being a vegetarian, such as alcohol and drug use. Finally, we asked if being vegetarian made an impact on your communities and the larger world around them. Is being vegetarian an active choice to be futuristic, idealistic, and optimistic?

Teen vegetarianism, we found, is not a frivolous decision.

As researchers we've always been curious about why teens choose to become vegetarians. Are you trying to make a statement? Make the world a better place? Make yourselves healthier than the older generation? Look better? Just be yourselves?

Question: *People become vegetarian for lots of different reasons. What is the most important reason that you became vegetarian?*
Replies:

"Knowing there is no need to kill a fellow creature to survive."

"I want to feel good about what I put into my body. I don't want to eat at the expense of an animal's life. And I want to eat healthy, wholesome food."

"I want to educate people about the harm they are doing by consuming meat. I eat a vegetarian diet in order to teach by example."

"I eat vegetarian because of my concern for animal rights. Vegetarians in general believe that using animals for food is cruel and wrong. There are also health benefits, including a lower rate of cancer, heart attacks, and obesity. Environmental factors are also important to vegetarians. It takes less than one quarter the amount of land to support a vegetarian than to support a meat eater. Religious beliefs may play a role in the decision. There are several religions that teach that vegetarianism is the right choice to make. With correct combinations of foods, vegetarians can easily get enough protein, vitamins, and minerals. In general, vegetarians can and do live long, happy lives, sometimes even more so than meateaters. In other words, there are a million reasons to choose vegetarianism."

health and longevity

There is a lot of evidence that vegetarians are healthier than nonvegetarians. Consider the following research findings:

- In a study of more than 70,000 people, death from heart disease was 30 percent lower in vegetarian men than in nonvegetarian men and 20 percent lower in vegetarian women than in nonvegetarian women.
- Studies in Germany and Finland suggest that people who eat no animal products may live an additional fifteen years compared to their animal-eating counterparts.
- Nonvegetarian men and women are nearly twice as likely to develop diabetes than vegetarian men and women. ·
- Vegetarians have lower blood pressure than nonvegetarians.
- Vegetarians are at a lower risk for obesity than nonvegetarians.
- In one study, those who ate meat for many years were more than three times as likely to develop signs of dementia (mental confusion) than Seventh-Day Adventists, whose religious beliefs do not permit them to eat meat.
- Nonvegetarians are twice as likely to have diverticulitis (a disease of the intestinal tract) than vegetarians.

"I didn't become a vegetarian to save the lives of cows and chickens. Cutting meat out of my diet just seemed like a good thing to try for a while. I feel so much healthier now, and I like that animals aren't suffering because of me."

Chat Room Posting:

"Hey! I am a vegetarian and have been since I was six. When people ask me why I don't eat meat I say because I do not want to eat a living thing. A lot of people say that plants are living, too. What can I say to that?"

Responses:

"Animals are sentient beings. They have feelings while plants do not."

"Plants are producers and animals are consumers. Plants die, decompose, and become part of the soil naturally. In the same way, our bodies use what we can of plants and then excrete the rest. This is a natural process. Animals we eat are often treated inhumanely before they are slaughtered for human consumption—this is not a natural process."

"When people ask me why I don't eat meat, I give them a well-informed response. I have memorized some statistics to spout as examples. Eating plants, though they are alive, doesn't harm my health or the environment."

vegetarian impact on the environment

Did you know?

- It takes about 25 gallons of water to produce a pound of wheat and 390 gallons to produce a pound of beef!
- An average steer consumes 16 pounds of grain and soy to produce 1 pound of steak on our plates!
- An acre of beans, peas and lentils can produce ten times the protein of an acre devoted to raising cattle!
- Grain consumed by American livestock could feed 800 million people!
- If the entire world switched to a vegan diet, our current food production would properly nourish 7 billion people. As it is now, only 4 billion of the world's 5.6 billion people are adequately nourished!

"I don't want to kill a living animal to eat and I don't want to eat a dead corpse/flesh."

Benefits Galore

Passionate, indeed. But the decision to become vegetarian goes beyond feeling good about the decision. How do you feel healthwise on a vegetarian diet? What other benefits are you experiencing? We posed the following question during our interviews and posted it on the Web.

Question: *What are the personal benefits of becoming a vegetarian?*

Replies:

"I was a vegetarian for three years, until recently, when I became a raw foodist. I am 13 years old. On a vegetarian diet, I feel better both mentally and physically. For example, my digestion has improved. Mentally, I have better focus and concentration. Becoming a vegetarian was also a healthy choice because it opened the door to many other valuable experiences that increased my overall well-being. Raw foodism has taken my vegetarianism to new heights; I am becoming increasingly aware of the power I have to influence my own health as well as the health of the planet!"

"I feel more moral as a vegetarian. I didn't feel good about myself as a meat eater, knowing animals were being harmed for my consumption. When I switched to vegetarianism, I also became involved with Animal Rights advocacy. Now I feel better about myself, morally, knowing I am educating people about the mistreatment of animals. My chi is more balanced; I feel as though I am living in harmony with nature. I feel healthier as a whole because of it."

"Vegetarianism has benefits for my personal life, because I have become increasingly aware of the different things that are around me. I've learned to enjoy everyday practices, like cooking, that I never before put any thought into. I think if people on a larger scale accepted that kind of practice, we could have a more thoughtful society. I don't know which would have to come first—more vegetarians or more awareness. But I do know that 'more awareness = more open-mindedness' and more acceptance of other peoples' differences."

"I've been introduced to new people and foods. I've made vegetarian friends, and I've discovered how good soybeans are! Also, studies show that vegetarians have longer endurance and faster reaction times. I think vegetarianism is especially cool because you don't have to worry about all that animal fat clogging up your arteries."

vegetarians and endurance

We were not able to find any evidence supporting the idea that vegetarians have longer endurance and faster reaction times. We do know, however, that competitive athletes can meet their nutritional needs on a vegetarian diet. If you are an athlete, make sure you are getting adequate amounts of protein, calcium, and iron.

"I have had a wealth of personal benefits from becoming vegan. My health took a dramatic upswing after the switch. I started to eat a diet comprised of raw nuts and raw nut butters, massive amounts of fruits, vegetables, whole sprouted grains, beans, beans, and more beans, tempeh, and seaweeds, and I started taking vitamins. My chronic migraines ceased. I had enough energy to become physically active, which has always been a dream of mine. My complexion became perfect. My hair is no longer oily at all. My eyes are bright and I receive comments from random strangers about how healthy I look. I actually can get out of bed in the morning and I no longer have mood swings. I also have become more aware of my role on this planet, animal suffering, natural health, and how to live longer and healthier. My mom even got in on the vegan thing and made the switch after she saw how good it made me feel. She has had chronic health problems and they are finally gone. The improvement was that dramatic. So I'd have to say that going vegan was a lifesaving event for me."

"I have a very picky system. When I ate meat, I would feel either sick to my stomach or lethargic. On the vegetarian diet I feel much healthier and have more energy to do things. Fruits and veggies are kind to my system. I also like to know that I am not contributing to the murder of animals. Even if I cannot control what other people do, I am sound with the fact that I have not harmed any other creature. I would like to remain in a peaceful mentality."

"I feel a lot healthier. I went to the doctor the other day and she told me that I was way healthy and my cholesterol levels are really low. And I feel like a stronger person because I have strong ideas about veganism. I've learned a lot about myself as I've made decisions about what I believe in."

The Turning Point

Question: *What made you decide to become vegetarian? Can you share your story of how you made the decision?*

Replies:

"I became a vegetarian after my sixth-grade zoology unit at school. I learned that every animal plays a big part in its ecosystem, and that if one species is killed off, the entire system suffers. I also have a new appreciation for what amazing creatures animals are; not just zebras and giraffes, but cows and pigs, too. I decided that my newfound 'Save the Animals' attitude clashed with eating meat, so I went vegetarian."

"I became vegetarian for economic reasons. When my parents stopped packing my lunch or giving me money to go eat with friends, I found out how expensive meat is. I can get a veggie sub for much cheaper than a sub with turkey or ham, and it tastes just as good."

"I became a vegetarian in seventh grade, because I thought it would help me lose weight. I stayed away from meat for a year, but I didn't get any thinner. Then I saw a documentary on TV about slaughterhouse conditions and the diseases that are subsequently passed on to the public, and I realized that vegetarianism is about a lot more than weight loss. Vegetarianism is a lifestyle choice; it's about respect for yourself and respect for the world around you."

"I became a vegetarian in order to avoid eating my mom's meat loaf. I couldn't tell her that I think her cooking is disgusting, so I told her I think *meat* is disgusting. Pretty soon I started to believe it. I would much rather eat fresh, brightly colored fruits and vegetables anyway. Though I didn't originally become a vegetarian for health reasons, that's why I've stayed one."

"My parents and I are vegetarians because of our religion. We are pagans, which means we live as naturally and as earth-friendly as possible. We believe that animals are divine. Animals deserve the same rights and freedom that humans do and therefore should not be kept in cages or used for our benefit."

"My aunt has always been a vegetarian, and she's known in our family as 'the healthy one' because of it. She is active, thin, happy, and vibrant. She is what inspired me to be a vegetarian.

"A few years ago, while on a bike trip with my family, we camped one night outside of a Spam factory. I thought about going vegetarian before that, and the smell of that place was the last straw. I realized workers have to spend entire days smelling that smell; I won't subject them to that torture just so I can eat meat (or fake meat!). And that's without considering the torture the animals go through!"

"All of us are influenced by the media. For example, I saw on the news that vegetarians are less likely to die of heart disease and cancer than meat eaters. I've also been reading about sustainable agriculture, and how many more people can be fed on grains than on cattle. Studies come out all the time, preaching the benefits of eating vegetarian. There seem to be so many reasons to eat a vegetarian diet, I don't see why not to."

a plant-based diet and cancer risk

Yes, vegetarianism can help reduce the risk of cancer. Research data show that vegetarians have a lower cancer rate overall than nonvegetarians. In particular, vegetarians have lower rates of prostate and colon cancer than meateaters.

"Once, when I was on a road trip with my family, I saw a dead raccoon at the side of the road. I saw my cat in that raccoon. My heart went out to the raccoon, just as it would if it were my cat, dead. I have a close relationship with all the animals that live with my family, and suddenly I realized that the raccoon was no different. And neither are the cows, chickens, and pigs that we eat for dinner. Now I don't eat meat, because I remember the love I have for my cat, and therefore all animals."

"For a long time, I wondered whether pets are different than animals we kill to eat. My curiosity wasn't overwhelming until I toured a biomedical lab and met a rat that was going to be studied under a microscope. A researcher sedated the rat, put the syringe into its stomach, and it let off a scream. There is something about that moment that has stayed with me forever. I felt so much compassion for the rat that I decided to stop eating meat. I realized then that pets aren't different at all from the animals that are killed for us to eat or the animals that are mistreated in the name of science."

"I have been a vegetarian for political reasons for a few years. I am disgusted with the meat industry, with cruelty to animals, and with government control in general. Recently, I decided that in order to live an honest, activist, liberal lifestyle, I have to be a freegan. Our society *wastes* such an incredible amount; I am able to live off its excess." [See page 15 for the definition of *freegan*.]

"Honestly, I don't know why I went vegetarian. But I do know that what started as a whim has developed into a passion. I had to learn a lot about nutrition in order to eat healthfully as a vegetarian, and that research grew to include animal rights and environmental issues. From everything I've learned, I am certain I made the best choice."

"I became a vegetarian after working in a vet's office. It didn't seem right to take care of animals all day and then go home and eat them for dinner. I read about factory farms and the mistreatment of dairy cows, and my reason for choosing vegetarianism soon switched from animal rights to ethics. I began eating a vegan diet to promote my new, ethical viewpoint. Not only do I believe it isn't right to eat animals, it isn't right to use animals for our benefit. That includes caging them for their eggs, milking them for their cream, shearing them for their wool, etc."

"I had been vegetarian for a year when I met a vegan girl. I was working at a bread store, and I used to bring her loaves of bread as little presents. She taught me about veganism, and how she couldn't eat certain bread because of the milk or eggs it contained. She was interested in human rights issues, so she talked a lot about poverty and the excessive lifestyle that most Americans live. She explained that ten vegans can live off the same amount of land as one meateater. I figured that if I became a vegan, and therefore consumed fewer natural resources, more people who live in poverty could be fed."

A Wholesome Lifestyle

Question: *What other habits or concerns do vegetarians share other than not eating meat? For example, do vegetarians in general refrain from certain lifestyle choices like drinking or using drugs or medication?*

Replies:

"I don't smoke or drink. Being a vegetarian means that I'm more aware of the harmful effects of what I put into my body. I don't want to breathe toxic smoke into my lungs, and alcohol ruins your liver."

"I refrain from drinking, smoking, doing drugs, and casual sex. Some of my vegetarian friends do all of these things, but I feel better when I don't. I am straight edge."

what is "straight edge"?

A straight edge is someone who refrains from smoking, drinking, and drug use. Sometimes the definition also includes abstaining from sexual activity and avoiding all animal products.

"I don't do drugs, and I rarely take medications. Most of the vegetarians I know don't extend their beliefs beyond their diet (they wear leather, use cosmetics tested on animals, etc.), but most teenage vegans and more active vegetarians only take medication when it's really necessary, not for miniscule problems like headaches or cramps. While drug and alcohol use is pretty much as diverse as it is with meat-eating teenagers, the teenage vegetarians I know are more environmentally aware and active than meat eaters."

"I have always thought that cigarettes, alcohol, drugs, and junk food are gross. Since becoming a vegetarian, and then a vegan, I am even more health conscious. I stay away from french fries and other greasy foods, even if they are vegan. I don't drink soda, either. I think my taste buds have changed since my eating habits have gotten healthier. I don't even like potato chips anymore. Call me a nerd, but I really love broccoli with fresh ginger!"

"I seldom drink alcohol or use drugs. I do use medications, but I try to limit it. I also make an effort to recycle, and I like to eat mostly organic foods. I know that when I get older and move out of my family's house I will be able to make even more of my own, environmentally friendly, choices."

"I sometimes do legal 'drugs' like smoking passion plant and catnip. They can give you a buzz, but not a potlike high. I quit smoking marijuana since becoming vegetarian, and I don't drink."

herbs as natural highs

Some young people have turned to herbal alternatives such as passion plant and catnip rather than using illegal substances such as marijuana. While there are mixed reports on the effects of smoking such herbs, many people claim that smoking passion plant, catnip, or valerian has a calming and sometimes hallucinogenic effect.

Unlike cigarettes and marijuana, however, there are few research studies to document the effects on the body of smoking these herbs. It can be assumed, though, that just like the smoke from cigarettes and marijuana, the smoke from these herbs may be harmful to the health of your lungs, mouth, and throat.

"I don't drink, smoke, or do drugs. I didn't become a vegetarian because of health reasons, but now that I am this healthy, why would I ruin it with all those toxic things?"

"I bike to work, which ends up being an hour every day. This is a healthy choice for myself and for the planet, because I get good exercise and my bike doesn't produce any air pollution. I am actually straight edge, though I don't call myself that. I don't like the way labels divide people into groups. I make healthy choices for myself, not to earn a title or to attract attention."

"There are many things in life that I realize I can live without. So I don't use shampoo or soap, and I don't buy things (like shoes) that I can otherwise find in dumpsters. I don't think it would be right for me to spoil myself by buying new things, when so many people are hungry. I wish that everyone had enough, instead of some people having too much and others nothing at all."

Question: *Who or what influenced you to become vegetarian? (Did a certain person tell you about it? Did you have an experience that made you become veggie?)*

Stories: We heard some great stories from you on what influenced teens to become vegetarian. Here are a few.

PURELY FOR THE HEALTH OF IT

"There wasn't a person who influenced my decision to become vegetarian. In fact, people around me look down on my choice. They argue that I must not be getting enough protein, B_{12}, or iron; they think my decision was an unhealthy one. I show them nutrition labels that prove I'm getting enough, and I explain that this is the healthiest decision I could have made for myself. And that's why I became a vegetarian in the first place—for the health of it. I decided that, now that I'm in high school, it's time to start thinking for myself and investing in my future. I figured that the health of my body is a good place to start.

"I first became a vegetarian after slowly giving up red meat, then chicken and turkey, then all seafood. I made the switch over about three months, and I did it purely for health reasons. I was known to say back then (I was fifteen) that I didn't have any problem with people killing animals for food; I just didn't eat meat because of my health. So obviously, I cared nothing for avoiding leather, fur, or other animal products in my clothing.

"As time went on and I took part in more and more e-mail lists, posted on message boards, and read books about vegetarianism, I felt a pull toward the vegan lifestyle. I started listening to the animal rights arguments that I used to ignore, and they made sense to me. I grew to believe that killing another living being was wrong, and I started to think about my own diet and lifestyle.

"I gave up dairy products a few months later and began to look at my wardrobe. What should I do? Throw out all my leather shoes and belts? Donate my fur-lined boots to the homeless? It all seemed pretty overwhelming and wasteful to me, so I started by simply promising myself never to buy another piece of clothing made from animals. Then I went through my closet.

"The hardest thing was deciding what to do with my Birkenstocks. But I'd sworn off leather, and I didn't need them—I just wanted them. I had worn the same pair of Birks for years, even asking my mom to have them resoled for me once when they wore out. It was hard to let them go, but because I had lots of other shoes, I gave them to a woman we knew who was really in need. That felt good, and it made it a little easier knowing they were going to a good cause. Then there were my belts and my purse. I only had one leather purse, so I used it for a few more months (till I got tired of answering questions about why I was vegetarian but carried a leather purse), then donated it to charity. For Christmas that year I asked my parents for money to buy some really cool nonleather belts and shoes. I must say, it felt good to finally be 'clean.'"

A SPECIFIC HEALTH ISSUE

"My interest in vegetarianism began when I found out I am lactose intolerant. It was so easy to give up dairy products that I decided to give up meat, too. I had always been concerned about cruelty to animals. Eventually, I went 100 percent vegan. I stayed away from lactose, gelatin, honey, etc. In fact, my diet was so restricted that I considered going macrobiotic. I don't work as hard to control my diet anymore. The vegan period of my life was just a phase; it was a way of expressing my individuality. I started to question whether I was eating how I wanted to, or how my family wanted me to. I think everybody explores different ways of eating at some point in their life. There is no one correct way, and it's fun to experiment. My time as a vegan was educational, too, because it forced me to learn about nutrition."

CURE FOR A PICKY EATER

"As a child I was a particularly picky eater. I refused cooked vegetables and any nonwhite meat that had a vein, or any other sign of life, running through it. In my house there was a rule that kids couldn't leave the table until their plates were clean. Needless to say, I was the last one in the kitchen every night.

"When I was sixteen I found a name for my 'selective' eating habits and told my parents, while they were washing pork chops down with gravy, that I was no longer going to eat meat. My father understood my refusal to eat animals as a snobby teenage declaration that I was too good for what he provided. My mom 'supported' my decision but would not prepare vegetarian meals and never stopped asking how I wanted my hamburger cooked.

"While being a vegetarian was in some ways an excuse to abstain from foods I didn't like, I stuck with it because I realized it was wrong to bring an animal into the world with the sole intention of killing him or her. However, I knew nothing about modern agribusiness and continued to consume eggs and dairy products, believing that they could be obtained without harming animals. Never once did I question whether we shouldn't be eating them, either.

"In order to better educate myself I decided to write my English 101 position paper in support of a vegan diet. I researched the impact animal products have on our health and was disgusted by what I learned. However, what was more nauseating to me was not what animals did to my body when I consumed them, but what I was paying someone to do to the animals before their milk and eggs arrived on my plate. Yet while I believed that animals didn't belong on our plates, I was worried I wouldn't be able to make the 'sacrifice' of being a vegan. 'What do vegans eat?' I wondered. I was determined to find out, so I printed out a list of animal ingredients and went through the food in our cupboard and the grocery store. After incorporating some new foods into my diet and learning that oftentimes I liked the cruelty-free versions better than the 'real thing,' I made a vow to go vegan for a month. I slipped a few times during the first few weeks, but instead of beating myself up, I acknowledged my mistake and promised myself that I wouldn't let it happen again. It didn't, and once I came to peace with my new diet, I decided to be a vegan for the rest of my life.

"Since becoming a vegan I haven't once felt deprived. In fact, I've discovered so many foods I love that I haven't had the chance to feel like I'm missing out on anything. While my parents still view me as a picky eater, I know it's not because I am stubborn and unwilling to try new things, but because I no longer view the animals they prepare as food.

"Paul McCartney once said, 'If slaughterhouses had glass walls, everyone would be a vegetarian.' I think it's my job to lead by example and make those walls a little more transparent."

A GRADUAL TRANSFORMATION

"'Would you like some roast beef, Courtney?' I cringed at my grandmother's words. I was at their house for Christmas, and I had recently become a vegetarian. I knew it was going to be hard, especially considering nobody in my family would dream of not being able to eat meat fewer than three times a day. I told her 'no' as politely as possible, explaining that I was now a vegetarian.

"Practically as soon as the word 'vegetarian' escaped my mouth, the entire family began ranting and raving about how I could not be a vegetarian:

> 'You'll get so sick.'
> 'What are you gonna do, live off of vegetables?'
> 'What are you going to do for protein? Huh?'

"I must say, it was not very simple at first. I got most of my support from my mom and from an organization called PETA (People for the Ethical Treatment of Animals). I heard about PETA from my stepmom, and I went to their website to learn more. There I read two different articles, one on pigs and slaughterhouses and the other on cows and leather. I was so disgusted with what I read that I gave away all the leather and suede that I owned.

greens, beans, and protein

Greens are only a fair source of protein, so you shouldn't count on them as your primary protein source. Cooked greens, such as spinach or collard greens, provide about 5 grams of protein per cup.

While green beans aren't a good source of protein, providing about 2 grams of protein per cup, other beans, such as northern, navy, or pinto, are great sources of protein, providing about 15 grams of protein per cup. An average teen weighing 125 pounds needs about 45 grams of protein per day.

"Maybe you, like most of my family, are wondering how I get protein. I eat tons of greens. If you want to go vegetarian, but think that means eating green beans and tofu three meals a day, then I suggest trying veggie burgers. Some of them actually taste a lot like meat, and most of them taste really good! If you like Mexican food, try tacos with tofu crumblers as a beef substitute. Or, if you prefer Thai and Chinese food, then you should like veggie-and-tofu stir-fries. They are so easy to make; they take less then ten minutes, and they are sooo good!"

WENT VEGAN COLD TURKEY

"It wasn't until I was sixteen that I heard about veganism. The first thing that came to my mind was, 'If you don't eat meat or dairy, what's left to eat!?' I thought it was crazy and I wondered, 'Where are you supposed to get your protein?'

"At the time, a friend gave me a little pamphlet called 'Why Vegan?' (Vegan Outreach; www.veganoutreach.com). I read it, and wow! I was convinced of how horrible everything was. I didn't see how anyone could read that and continue to eat meat!

"I remember the last thing I ate before becoming vegan: three pieces of pepperoni pizza. That was my favorite meal at the time. The next morning, I woke up and started my life as a vegan. I think of it as 'going vegan cold turkey.' I'm sure my parents thought it was a phase I was going through, much like my 'crazy hair' phase and my piercing phase, both of which I still have not 'outgrown.' It was difficult the first year. Being such a 'baby vegan,' I didn't know what half the ingredients were; which were vegan and which were not. I was aware of whey and lactose, but I'd often buy vegetarian cheeses thinking they were also vegan. I didn't realize it just meant 'rennet-free,' and I had no idea what casein was.

"I knew the basics, I guess. I knew eggs were pure evil, yet, being a cookie lover, I found them hard to avoid. They seemed to be in all the top brand cookies. A book that helped me out also was *The New Farm Vegetarian Cookbook.*"

know your whey, casein, and rennet

Whey, casein, and rennet are ingredients derived from dairy products.

Whey is the watery part of milk that separates from the curd, and casein is a protein found in the milk of all mammals. Casein is occasionally found in bread, gum, medicines and vitamins, canned tuna fish, chicken broth, and chocolate. Rennet is an enzyme derived from the stomach of slaughtered calves and added to milk to coagulate it to make cheese products.

Cheeses can be made with rennet from fungal or bacterial sources or genetically altered microorganisms. These are not animal products, and so the cheeses are truly vegetarian.

DETERMINED—DESPITE LITTLE SUPPORT

"During the summer of 2001, my co-worker—who was a vegetarian—told me a lot about veganism. I remember I was eating gummi candy when she told me what gelatin and beeswax really were. I was horrified and threw away my gummi candy immediately. I decided to become vegan and began avoiding animal products. It surprised me that I was able to give up dairy so fast, considering my love for ice cream! I had more trouble giving up chicken, seafood, and eggs. Also, it was a pain to check the nutrition labels on *everything.*

"The only person who supports me is my twin sister, who is also vegan. My parents refuse to buy me food, my school doesn't care about my needs, and my so-called friends are totally inconsiderate. One time my 'friend' pulled me aside and said, 'Please stop what you're doing. It's not healthy at all and you're just going to ruin your body. Someone I know got very sick when she replaced dairy milk with soy milk.' I thought, 'Well, that person was probably allergic to soy milk!' I feel absolutely great and healthier ever since I became vegan. Just knowing that I'm not hurting animals and that I'm helping the environment makes me feel a hundred times better."

how do you milk a soybean?

Soy milk is a nondairy milky liquid made from soybeans. Soy milk is made by boiling soy beans and then squeezing out the liquid. Soy milk can be poured over your breakfast cereal and used to replace milk in recipes. Here is how soy milk and skim milk compare nutrient-wise:

NUTRIENT	SOY MILK (1 cup)	SKIM MILK (1 cup)
Calories	81 calories	86 Calories
Protein	7 grams	8 grams
Calcium	10 mg	302 mg

Some soy milk is fortified with calcium and is a better soy choice for teens.

A MOOING STORY

"About two years ago, something inside of me snapped. Suddenly I felt sorry for the animals who had to die because I was hungry for a hamburger or taco. I went online to research cruelty to animals, and I am forever glad that I did. I had no idea that they are treated so poorly.

"I found some absolutely horrid pictures of what happens in factory farms. I grew up in farm country and had been to the processing department of a slaughterhouse. It grossed me out, but I thought it was normal. Though I lived nearby, I never saw or heard what the animals go through on the 'farms.' On the day that I saw those pictures and read that information about what happens to animals in slaughterhouses, I went vegetarian.

"The first couple of weeks, I slipped and ate some tacos. I felt horrible afterwards. Your body is so attuned to craving meat, your body is saying yes, but your heart and mind are saying no. It was a tug-of-war for me. The smell of meat made me crave it so badly that my mouth would water and I would do everything I could not to indulge. Now the smell of meat makes me physically ill. When I feel like caving in and eating meat, I go back to those websites to look at the pictures and read the facts. The cruelty depicted always makes me want to persevere.

"To tell you the truth, before I was vegetarian, I believed the common cliché that vegans are radical human rights activists; the raging violent lunatics who always shove their views down everyone else's throats. Now that I am a vegan, I have caught more flack from meat/dairy consumers than I have dished out to anyone. I honestly think vegans make some people feel guilty. They realize that eating meat is wrong and that they aren't strong enough to give it up, so they harass me out of guilt. I can't think of any other justification to attack a vegan."

A COOL MOM HELPS

"I suppose it could be said that my upbringing predisposed me to vegetarianism. I grew up in the 'cheese state' of Wisconsin. Cows were everywhere. I grew up on a peninsula in a very small town of about 1,000 people. I lived in a log cabin, played in the woods, and led a pretty natural life. My mom was paranoid about raising her kids correctly. She breast-fed me till I was two. My baby food was all homemade, usually pureed or strained vegetables from our organic garden. We were discouraged from eating a lot of meat. One chicken breast was split three ways between my two sisters and me for dinner. We were never forced to drink milk. I generally went along with whatever my mom served, but I drew the line at zucchini!

"When I was twelve, I read a book promoting veganism and plant-based nutrition. It left a lasting impression on me. I decided that I would become a vegetarian when I was an adult. I saw no reason to make the change immediately because I did not feel that my health was in any danger at the tender age of twelve. However, sometime during my sixteenth year, I came across an article discussing how the decisions that we make when we're younger regarding our lifestyle affect the quality of our lives later in life. I made the decision to move toward a more plant-based diet immediately. I was suffering from severe migraines at the time, and I thought a healthier diet might help.

"I decided at sixteen to move away from processed foods and make the switch to a mostly vegan eating pattern. I say 'mostly' because I do not believe that it is possible to be completely vegan in this life, due to the construct of our society. My mom was very supportive, which is not typical when a teen makes this announcement. She gladly bought me nondairy milks, blocks of tofu, whole-grain breads, and helped me find books on vegetarian cooking. She tried my cooking creations no matter how weird the ingredients (like seaweed). I wreaked havoc in her kitchen but she understood as long as I cleaned up after myself! Once she even bought one of every vegetable in the store. Not a month passes that she doesn't complement me on my healthy lifestyle. I have been very lucky to have her support.

"I am indebted to the Internet resources and the wealth of cookbooks that are available to those aspiring to eat lower on the food chain. My health did improve noticeably. Since altering my eating pattern I have more energy, the intensity and frequency of my headaches has decreased, and I've learned valuable information about nutrition and health in the process. A little bit of green on your plate does a lot of good.

"As for as my transition to meatless eating, I have to say that it has been a neverending process toward better cooking on my part. Some of my favorite veggie foods are rice dream, Luna bars, Amy's organic frozen entrees, Ezekiel 4:9 bread, stir-fried tempeh and tofu, vegetable sushi, lentil soup, and, of course, peanut butter and banana sandwiches. I even like zucchini now. I also take a multivitamin and a spoonful of flaxseed oil everyday, to make sure that I'm getting what I need. I am 100 percent healthy."

"The most valuable thing that I learned from being a part of the public school system is the absolute necessity of having an individual, separate life away from the one you lead at school. I went to a very small school that lacked diversity. Lack of diversity didn't mean just a lack of minorities. It also meant that if you didn't think the same as everybody else, then you were subtly ostracized by students and teachers.

"People started to notice when I wouldn't join in the class efforts to bash Asians. I was deemed 'snotty' because I wouldn't join them in the woods after school to drink out of a keg. I was called a 'bitch' because I wouldn't swallow pills that they had bought from their cousin's sister's uncle that had promised them a high. I would hear daily 'you're not ugly so why haven't you had sex?'

"This was nothing, however, compared to the hostility that I experienced when I decided at sixteen to follow a vegetarian/vegan lifestyle. Of particular nastiness was a certain teacher. Not a day went by that she didn't harass me. I was never one of the militant types that passed out brochures or regaled people with facts on cholesterol, etc. (I saved that for people I cared about, like my family.) I simply wanted to be me. Instead of teaching her class, she would hold ice cream and cake parties every third day. She would constantly offer me nonvegan candy, cake, and ice cream.

"I find it interesting that the same type of behavior began to be directed at my younger sister when she started to bring healthier vegetarian lunches to her elementary school. The children appeared to have some sort of homing device set to detect nondairy, nonmeat food. It was tough to convince her to stay constant in her manner of eating. The fact that the same thing happened to me in high school made me laugh. I couldn't believe that I still had people bothering me about my lunch in the twelfth grade! It's become second nature for me to handle being constantly under attack just for existing the way I wish to exist.

"I have to say that I am glad that I am different. I don't plan to change. I am just worried about the world that my children grow up in. I hope that common sense will be dispensed more liberally than it is now."

Hope for a Better World

So many of the teens we talked with and whose stories we read were very concerned about the environment and the way the world is evolving. This theme is central to the vegetarian philosophy. It is comforting to know that people are worried about their planet at an early age and are doing something about it. This theme led to the following question.

Question: *How does the fact that you are vegetarian impact the world around you (think locally and globally)?*

Replies:

"I don't really think my being vegan makes much of an impact right now. I have yet to 'convert' anyone, although I've gotten some people to consider it and try it out. I've also opened people up to the fact that animal rights activism does exist, and so do 'crazy' vegans. I don't think my involvement is saving many animals. Over time, though, I know that choosing vegan will make a difference. As more and more people start, our efforts will add up. A vegan lifestyle has a smaller impact on the environment, because fewer resources are expended in grain production than in meat production. Later in life I plan on going to law school or running for political office. Then I can use my power and influence to encourage change on a larger scale."

"Chickens are kept in horrible conditions; they are kept in small cages, packed so tightly that they don't have room to move. Sometimes they die simply as a result of their living conditions. It's brutal. They are injected with synthetic hormones that come into our bodies when we eat their meat. We are also at risk for the diseases the animals may have contracted as a result of their living conditions. The environment suffers, too. I hate to think about all the methane pollution released by cattle. There are so many problems with the mass production of meat, and yet the industry keeps telling us to buy more of it—to eat more of it."

"I don't think you make a big impact as one person. Change comes with numbers. I don't think I am saving any animals from slaughter, but I am not participating in the violence and exploitation. However, I know that people around me are eating less meat and are more willing to look into vegetarianism due to me educating them. So, maybe I am making more of an impact than I believe."

"And what do I bring to the community? A lot. Vegetarians not only care about the lives of animals, but human rights issues and environmental issues, too. We bring a greater understanding of all these things to our community."

Summing It Up

- Many teens become vegetarians because of their concern about eating and harming animals.

- Many also become vegetarians to improve their health or manage their weight.

- Some became vegetarians because of religious or political beliefs.

- Some turn to vegetarianism through the influence of others.

- Most feel vegetarianism could make a difference in the world and the environment if more people become vegetarian.

dealing with
carnivorous parents

SO, HOW WILL YOUR PARENTS REACT WHEN YOU TELL THEM YOU'VE COME OUT OF THE PANTRY CLOSET? WELL, IT MAY NOT BE AS BAD AS YOU THINK.

AT LEAST THAT IS THE IMPRESSION WE GOT FROM MANY OF THE YOUNG PEOPLE WE TALKED TO. THOUGH EXPERIENCES WILL VARY, YOU CAN EXPECT THAT YOUR DECISION WILL BE TREATED WITH AT LEAST SOME RESISTANCE, AND NATURALLY, A LOT OF PARENTAL CONCERN. ARMED WITH THE BEST INFORMATION AND APPROACH, HOWEVER, YOU SHOULD BE ABLE TO BRING A RELUCTANT PARENT AROUND TO YOUR WAY OF THINKING.

These stories and our professional responses to common parental concerns should help you break the ice.

Expect the Unexpected

You think you know your parents well, but you may not get a warm reaction when you come to them with the idea of converting to something perceived as radical as vegetarianism. The answers that follow will help you plan your own approach.

Question: *How did your parents react to your becoming vegetarian?*

Replies:

"I think my parents reacted like most other families do to their teens: 'Oh—it's just a fad.' At first, my parents weren't well educated about vegetarianism. They were worried about my health, and they didn't understand why I suddenly wanted to change my eating habits. As time passed and I learned more about the vegetarian diet, they began to understand that I am actually healthier as a vegetarian than I was on a meat-eating diet. My parents also worried that vegetarianism would lead inevitably to veganism; they thought once I started to restrict my diet, I would get stricter and stricter. I researched health benefits and vegan protein sources, and when they realized I was making smart, informed choices, they began to respect me more and more. They claim to be too old to make the switch to vegetarianism themselves, otherwise they'd be right there with me!"

"In my family, vegetarianism was a joke and a major point of contention. We honestly had fights at the dinner table about which nutrients I was missing out on. So, I had to do tons of research to prove to my mom that I was being healthy and living a good lifestyle for a growing teen. Eventually, my vegetarianism became a good thing for the entire family. My little sisters really look up to me, so now they are also saying 'I don't want to eat meat anymore.' It's exciting to see the influence I have over the people around me. My mom is still upset, though. She does all the cooking, and having three vegetarians in the house means she has to learn new recipes and even prepare two different meals at once. I've tried to help. I'll tell her, 'If you make this vegetarian meal, I'll cook one meal a week.' She likes that! But I still have to do all the vegetarian shopping, because she doesn't know what we eat."

"I was teased a lot by family and friends, but that didn't stop me. My mom was worried about whether or not I would get enough protein and nutrients, but her worries are based on her misconceptions. I think I can get everything I need from a plant-based diet."

the nutrients issue

You can come very close to finding all the nutrients that you need from a totally plant-based diet. But if you are vegan, it is nearly impossible to get the vitamin B_{12} that you need because vitamin B_{12} is produced from microorganisms living in animal tissues.

Vitamin B_{12} is important because it is involved in cell division, red blood cell formation, the functioning of the nervous system, and the metabolism of essential amino acids and fatty acids. Since B_{12} has a role in cell division, it is exceptionally important during times of growth and development—like the child and teenage years. Teens ages fourteen to eighteen and adults need 2.4 micrograms of vitamin B_{12} daily.

A deficiency in vitamin B_{12} can lead to anemia, damage to the nervous system, mental confusion, and numbness and tingling in fingers and toes.

Vegans need to take a B_{12} supplement or nutritional yeast fortified with vitamin B_{12}. Fortified nutritional yeast can be sprinkled on salads or used in recipes. If you choose to use yeast as your B_{12} source, make sure that it is fortified with B_{12} (Red Star T-6635+ is a reliable source), and don't consume more than 3 tablespoons daily. If you are a lacto-ovo vegetarian, you will get the B_{12} that you need in eggs or dairy products.

MAJOR HEALTH ISSUE

"My dad said right away, 'Okay, I work with other dads who have teenage daughters, and every single one of them has gone through their vegetarian phase. You'll last a week—two weeks tops.' He was positive I was going to grow out of it. And then, when they realized I was serious, they became concerned about my health. They called a nutritionist, who told them that vegetarianism is very healthy if you're smart about it. Then they thought, 'It's those vegans who are very 'unhealthy.' They were convinced that as long as I ate dairy and eggs for protein, I would be okay. I believed them. I stayed a vegetarian until I was convinced that vegan protein sources are just as good, if not better. So, when I went vegan, my parents were seriously concerned about my health.

At that time, I was suffering from an eating disorder. I was trying to figure out why I sometimes felt guilty when I ate. I started thinking it was all tied together—that maybe I felt guilty eating because I felt bad about eating animals. The dietitian and my parents all said, 'You're just trying to control how you eat in a different way. If this is unhealthy, you can't do it.' And the dietitian refused to help me. I pleaded with her to *please* give me information, and she said, 'You can't do it. We won't let you do it. You can't.' Eventually I stopped seeing her and went vegan on my own. My parents are still worried about me, but I feel less guilty about eating now that I know I'm not harming any animals in the process. I have more energy now, too, both mentally and physically."

My mom was worried about my health and my social life. She thought that veganism would turn me into an outcast; that people would think *I* was weird because my diet is 'weird.' She was concerned that vegans hate people who use animal products. She also worried that veganism is an eating disorder, because of the control and obsession involved in such a restricted diet. Mostly, my mom was threatened by the strong statement I was making through food; she thought I was being a rebel. She didn't think I would ever compromise on anything ever again. My parents claim to support my decision, but they tell me frequently that it's going to stunt my growth."

parental concern: vegetarians and eating disorders

Eating disorders are a valid concern for teen vegetarians, unfortunately. Our research shows that there is an association between eating disorders and vegetarianism in teens. In a study conducted in Minnesota schools, we found that teens who said they were vegetarian were twice as likely to engage in some kind of unhealthy weight-control practice, three times as likely to report intentional vomiting, and nearly eight times as likely to report laxative use. So it appears that some teens with eating disorders do try to disguise a change in eating habits by saying that they've become vegetarian.

Becoming a vegetarian, however, does not put anyone at risk for developing an eating disorder. Also, vegetarianism does *not* cause eating disorders.

Take a look at chapter 7 for more information on eating disorders and weight issues for vegetarian teens.

NOT MUCH SUPPORT

"My mom grew up on a farm, raising animals for meat. When I decided to go vegetarian, she thought I didn't respect her. It took her two years to make peace with my choice, but she finally came around and started buying and cooking vegetarian food. Then, I shocked and upset her all over again by becoming vegan. She thought I was being too radical and didn't understand why I felt the need to rebel. After a few months, she began to understand what a healthy, rational decision I had come to. She doesn't agree with it, though. She doesn't see anything unethical about using animals for food or clothing. My mom accepts what I'm doing because she knows she can't convince me to turn back. My grandpa was the only supportive family member. He doesn't care about what I eat, as long as I'm healthy and happy. My mom, who's on the Atkins diet, doesn't understand why I'd want to *remove* meat from my diet. Atkins claims the more meat, the better. I explain to her that I'm not vegetarian in order to lose weight, I'm vegetarian because 'meat is murder.' That statement alone gets me in a lot of trouble with my dad's family, who is Lebanese. Their diet is all chicken or steak, and potatoes. By cutting the meat out of my diet, I am breaking with cultural norms."

"My parents are divorced, so I get a different reaction to my vegetarianism depending on whose house I'm at. My mom is totally cool about it, because she used to be a vegetarian herself. It's my dad who gives me a hard time. He sees my choice as an annoyance; he can no longer make the same old meals he's been preparing for years. My vegetarianism is forcing *change*, which, he claims, makes his life more difficult. He needs to realize that *change* is precisely the reason that I'm doing this. I know my whole family will be healthier on a vegetarian diet. The ironic thing is that we never ate a lot of meat in the first place, so the changes aren't very dramatic. I think my dad is upset that I'm making choices for myself. He doesn't want to see his baby girl grow up! At first, my parents thought vegetarianism was a new way to rationalize picky eating. They tried preparing meat in new ways they thought I would like and insisted that I try everything. I consistently refused; admittedly, I was obnoxiously stubborn. After they realized I was serious, they started replacing chicken with tofu or fish with seitan. They used meat alternatives in all their new recipes! Now our kitchen is stocked with healthy, vegetarian food. (I won!)"

THEY WERE WAY OKAY!

"My parents have been really supportive. We do our grocery shopping at co-ops, so there are a lot of fresh veggies and vegetarian protein sources available. My dad and I have a ton of fun with food. Every weekend, we go to the co-op and make a point of choosing new foods in the deli case. Then we take it all to a sunny place and have a picnic. If it's raining, or too cold to be outside, we go to the conservatory. The conservatory is a big, indoor garden/greenhouse where it feels like summer even in the dead of winter. My dad and I love to eat fresh, vegetarian food while surrounded by flowers and plants. It makes us feel in harmony with nature."

what is a food co-op?

Cooperatives are organizations that are owned and run by many people in a community. Many cities and towns have cooperative natural foods grocery stores to which community members buy a membership. Owning a membership, in this case, actually means that a person owns part of the grocery store. He or she has the right to elect cooperative board members, vote on company issues, and often get bargains on groceries and other nonfood natural items.

Natural food cooperative grocery stores often provide educational classes on food preparation and other health issues and are active in community development. It is a great place to learn about vegetarian food and to meet other vegetarians.

"My parents eat a lot of meat, but they are still very supportive. At home they always make sure I get a balanced, vegetarian meal. If we go to a restaurant without anything I can eat, they ask our server if the kitchen can prepare something special. More often than not, restaurants are willing to accommodate me. I think as the number of vegetarians increases, places will have more and more options for us."

"My family has been surprisingly supportive, considering we are Native Americans. Hunting is a big part of our culture, so obviously we eat a lot of meat. Luckily, eating naturally and respecting the earth is also a big part of our culture. In that sense, vegetarianism isn't so bizarre."

PARENTS BECAME CONVERTS

"The day my mom served veggie corn dogs was the day we all became vegetarians. Those corn dogs were so good, and so much healthier, that none of us saw any reason to go back to real meat."

"My parents went to Europe for six months when they first married. They didn't have much money then, so they traveled around eating beans and toasted cheese sandwiches. That cheap, vegetarian diet stuck until a hunter friend gave them enough venison for us to live on for months. We *loved* that meat and began to buy other meat products. My sister was the one who reinitiated vegetarianism. She never liked the looks of that slaughtered deer in our freezer. She proposed a family switch to veganism, in the name of animal rights. To make a long story short, we all made the change. Now the only time we have meat products in the house is when my mom accidentally buys bread with eggs in it. In that case, we give the loaf away to a food shelf or a friend."

SOME TOUGH COOKIES HERE

"My mother is *seriously* upset about my decision to go vegetarian. She has repeatedly said that it's the worst thing that could've happened to our family. This seems to be an excessively dramatic reaction to my eating habits, especially considering two of her brothers died in Vietnam. I've tried to explain myself to her, but she won't listen and she won't support me. I have to make all my own meals."

"I come from a "meat and potatoes" family in Wisconsin—the kind of family who thinks vegetarians only exist in the movies. Whatever my mom put on the table, we had to eat. And we couldn't get up until we cleaned our plates. I *never* liked meat. When I moved away to go to college, I could make my own food choices for the first time. Naturally, I stopped eating what I didn't like, because my parents weren't there to force it down my throat anymore. They found out I wasn't eating meat at college and accused me of trying to lose weight or trying to be trendy. They didn't believe that I never liked meat in the first place. But now, because I've kept the vegetarian diet up, and because they can see how healthy I am, they accept it 100 percent."

"My mom honestly thought I was kidding. She continued cooking a lot of meat and putting it right in front of my face, and I continuously refused to eat it. Only after I started losing weight did she become concerned. She realized I wasn't consuming enough calories or getting my daily vitamins and minerals, so she started cooking more vegetables, beans, and rice. Eventually she began buying tofu and other soy products. My weight is up, and I successfully convinced her vegetarianism is no joke."

parental concern: weight loss

A lot of teens (and their parents) are under the misconception that they will automatically lose weight if they become vegetarian, but that is not necessarily so. Weight loss occurs when you use or burn up more energy (calories) than you consume.

You can easily be a vegetarian and still eat more calories than you burn up, especially if you are not physically active. For example, you can be a vegetarian and still:

- Drink calorie-dense, nutrient-poor soft drinks (150 calories per 12-ounce can)
- Eat a whole bag of potato chips at a sitting (600 calories per 4-ounce bag)
- Stuff yourself on veggie burgers (two veggie burgers with veggie mayonnaise, bun, lettuce, tomato, and cheese = 940 calories)
- Eat lots of cheese (100 calories an ounce)

None of these practices are part of a healthful diet, vegetarian or otherwise. Vegetarians, however, are at lower risk for being obese than nonvegetarians, and a healthy vegetarian diet includes all the elements of a diet designed to reach and maintain a healthy weight. Healthy vegetarians choose from a wide variety of foods, eat plenty of fruits and vegetables, and are conscientious about the foods and beverages they put in their mouths. If they really care about their bodies and the environment, they will be physically active, too. Winning habits for a healthy weight!!

"No one in my family is supportive, and they aren't afraid to be vocal about it. My grandfather accused me of being 'stupid.' Every time I buy vegetarian alternatives, or order a vegetarian meal at a restaurant, my mom grumbles: 'This is so stupid. I don't know why you do this.' Despite all this negativity, I remain obstinate. *I* know why I do this: for my health, for the environment, and for animal rights."

"My mom doesn't take my vegetarianism seriously. She thinks that it's something I want to learn about but not necessarily do. She has helped me buy books on the subject, as well as new foods, but she continues to serve me meat. It's almost like cutting all meat out of my diet is too radical of a concept to even consider."

recommended reading

Some of our favorite references for vegetarians and vegans are:

The New Becoming Vegetarian: The Essential Guide to Adopting a Healthy Vegetarian Diet by Brenda Davis and Vesanto Melina

Becoming Vegan: The Complete Guide to Adopting a Healthy Plant-based Diet by Brenda Davis and Vesanto Melina.

Vegan: The New Ethics of Eating by Eric Marcus.

"I started wanting to be a vegetarian in sixth grade, but my parents wouldn't let me. They said I didn't know enough about it to do it healthfully. In actuality, I think they were scared that I was turning into a rebel and would soon dye my hair green or pierce my nose. Now that I'm in tenth grade, still have my natural hair color, and still want to be a vegetarian, they're cool with it."

"My mom was antivegetarian for a while. When I was in elementary school, my family ate a lot of meat. When my brother became a vegetarian we cut back, and then I became a vegetarian and we cut back even more. Then, when my parents got divorced, my dad became a vegan—he just went all the way."

COULDN'T CARE LESS

"My parents don't pay any attention to how I eat. They have never asked me why I'm a vegetarian, or how I get my protein, vitamins, and minerals. Now that I've learned so much about nutrition, I've noticed their carnivorous diet is unbalanced. For example, my parents don't eat any green leafy vegetables. The only salad they eat is iceberg lettuce, which doesn't have much nutritional value. I'm going to start giving them unsolicited advice!"

"My mom cooks extra meals without complaining. I make sure she knows how grateful I am, especially because some of my vegetarian friends have unsupportive parents. She makes eating meat-free easy."

"My parents don't care unless I refuse to eat something with chicken stock. They insist that chicken stock is not chicken and that I am being ridiculous and obsessive when I refuse to eat a soup with chicken-stock base. How tough is it to use vegetarian stock instead? You can buy vegetarian bouillon cubes!"

Question: *What are some specific things that happened in your home when you went vegetarian?*

Replies:

THE TRICKS THEY TRY!

"My dad never cooks. So, when he made lasagna and insisted it was meatless, I was happy to eat it. I had no reason to think he was lying, and I wanted to support his cooking efforts. One bite, though, and I knew the meat wasn't tofu crumblers. I asked them why they tried to trick me; they said they wanted me to see that the sky wouldn't fall if I ate a little beef. Needless to say, I felt like they were being disrespectful."

"My mom and I have the same fight over and over again. She buys sausage and pepperoni pizzas even though she knows I won't eat the meat. Then, when I pick the meat off, she accuses me of wasting it. The same thing happens every time she makes spaghetti. She puts ground beef in the sauce and claims to have forgotten that I am a vegetarian. When I pick the meat out, she gets angry."

"My parents are absolutely crazy to think I don't know a hamburger when I see one. They try to pass them off as veggie burgers at every summer barbeque. It's true that some brands taste more like beef than others, but there are definite differences. No part of a veggie burger is ever pink."

parental concern: iron

The worry here probably comes from the notion that the only source of iron is red meat. Some parents of vegetarians worry that the switch to a diet without meat means their teen won't get enough iron and may become anemic.

Certain vegetables, however, do contain iron, a type call "nonheme" iron. (Meat contains "heme" iron.) Nonheme iron works in the same way as heme iron—it builds healthy blood. This means that we do not need to eat blood to make blood!

Males and females who are thirteen or younger need about 8 milligrams of iron every day. Female teenagers ages fourteen to eighteen need 15 milligrams a day and males need 11 milligrams a day. Some particularly good sources of iron in a plant-based diet include:

FOOD	AMOUNT	IRON CONTENT (mg)
Fortified Cream of Wheat	3/4 cup	9-11
Fortified dry cereal	1/2 cup	4-18
Wax beans, canned or cooked	1/2 cup	3
Lentils, cooked	1/2 cup	3
Hummus	1/2 cup	2

MIXED MESSAGES

"My mom doesn't have time to accommodate my vegetarianism. She doesn't want to read labels to find out what's safe for me to eat, and she certainly doesn't want to cook anything special for me. So I have a weekly food budget. I do all my own grocery shopping and all of my own cooking. This added responsibility gives me a taste of what it'll be like to live on my own. It also makes me think hard about my choice to be a vegetarian, because I have to work for it."

"I am a vegan. My diet is really easy to follow, because I love fruit and other 'rabbit food,' as my family calls it. In my daily life, I don't run into any problems caused by veganism. People around me are very supportive; I was overweight before I went vegan, and now weight management is relatively easy. The only time that my diet is an issue is on holidays, when my entire family congregates and eats traditional holiday foods. Nothing at Christmas is vegan. Even the vegetables are covered in butter. My family is unwilling to change on those days, arguing that traditions are more important than accommodating my strict diet. Every year my grandmother makes what used to be my favorite dessert: Jell-O cake. She doesn't understand that vegans don't eat gelatin."

"My parents use every rule I break as a segue into why vegetarianism is a bad choice. For example, what starts as an argument over a broken curfew Saturday night turns into a discussion of the lack of iron sources in my diet. My mom desperately wants me to start eating chicken in order to replace the red meat that I refuse to eat. Basically, every meal and every rule I break is an excuse for an argument."

Question: *Do you usually cook for yourself or does your family cook for you?*

Replies:

YOU'RE ON YOUR OWN, PAL

"Our main course is meat every single night. That means that I eat a lot of vegetable side dishes, rice, and bread. My mom accommodates me a little, by leaving the bacon out of the au gratin potatoes and stuff like that, but she never cooks a full vegetarian meal. I got tired of eating only side dishes, so I've learned to cook a few vegetarian things. Honestly, it took me a long time to find new, exciting foods and even longer to learn how to cook them. Sometimes I make dinner for my whole family, but it doesn't usually go over well. They don't understand that being healthy means getting used to nutritious foods.

They don't believe they can learn to love things like turkey sand-wiches without the turkey (better yet, with soy turkey!)"

"My mom doesn't let me cook for the family, because she thinks I'll ruin the food. If you call leaving the meat out of spaghetti sauce ruining, then I guess I'm guilty. Anyway, my parents have gotten into the habit of adding the meat to the meal last, so that I can take my portion and add fake meat instead. I add textured protein or tofu to almost every-thing. If they barbeque, I throw a slab of marinated firm tofu on the grill or make my own vegetable kebabs. Sometimes I catch my dad eyeing my food, wishing Mom would let me cook for once!"

parental concern: cooking right

There are many vegetarian cookbooks for teens. One with very simple recipes is *The Starving Students' Vegetarian Cookbook* by Dede Hall.

The following cookbooks aren't just for teens, but they are some of our favorites:

Moosewood Restaurant's Low-Fat Favorites by The Moosewood Collective.

The Complete Soy Cookbook by Paulette Mitchell.

Laurel's Kitchen by Laurel Robertson, Carol Flinders, and Bronwen Godfrey.

"My family is divided. My dad refuses to touch, let alone ingest, any-thing that is soy. (He kisses my mom, who drinks soy milk. Does that count?) I don't understand how some people are scared of an inno-cent soybean but have no fear of bloody flesh. There's no logic to carnivores. I have two younger brothers; the oldest shares my dad's tough guy, flesh-eating persona, and the youngest drinks soy with my mom. To please everyone, Mom cooks two meals every night. I think Dad should cook the meat meal, and Mom and I should cook vege-tarian. Then maybe the carnivores would be open to soybeans!"

"My mom insures I have a vegetable and vegan bread at dinner, but it's never a full meal. I don't have time to cook more for myself, because I'm involved in after-school activities. I have to compensate by eating more during the day, so I pack nuts and energy bars for snacks."

"I've convinced my mother that veganism is a sure way to lose those extra pounds, so she's supportive. Together we've found a lot of cool new recipes. We love to make homemade hummus and then dip veggies or pita, or use it as a sandwich spread. Hummus is easy to make, and you can flavor it with all different things like garlic, lemon juice, olives, or cumin."

"I cook 95 percent of my own meals. My dad is a vegetarian, too, so he often eats with me. My mom, on the other hand, thinks it's horrible that I've stopped eating meat. She discourages my behavior by refusing to touch anything I cook and refusing to cook anything special for me."

SEPARATE MEALS TOGETHER

"My family very rarely asks me to cook my own food. And I do always eat with them. My dad does all the cooking at home and he is really nice about it. He and my mom want me to explore my own beliefs. They don't go out of their way, but they always have veggie burgers in the fridge. They even buy different brands and flavors, so that I don't get bored. Also, we eat less meat than we did before I became a vegetarian. Now, if they're having meat loaf or hamburgers, I eat a veggie burger. Or if my dad makes something that's easy to divide into two batches, he leaves one meatless. Lasagna is my favorite food, so I always make sure he leaves the meat out of part of it!"

"My family loves Mediterranean food. It's healthy because of the fresh vegetables and herbs, and because olive oil is a source of 'good'

(monounsaturated) fat. Mediterranean cooking also has so many interesting ingredients that it doesn't need meat to give food its flavor. For example, we put feta cheese, olives, sundried tomatoes, and/or pine nuts on lots of foods (rice, salads, pasta, etc.) to make it exciting."

lasagna you can love

Lasagna lovers note: Tofu is a great substitute for ground beef. Recipes for tofu lasagna can be found online and in vegetarian cookbooks. Some feature tofu as a substitute for ricotta cheese but still include mozzarella, while others are completely vegan.

As a general rule of thumb, tofu can be crumbled together with garlic powder, oregano, basil, salt and pepper, and even bread crumbs to give good texture and flavor for your favorite lasagna recipe. We recommend layering cooked lasagna noodles, fresh organic tomato sauce, spinach and mushrooms or any other grilled or sautéed vegetables that you like, and the tofu mixture mentioned here. It makes a delicious vegan dinner.

"We only sit down to dinner together about five times a year. On those days, I eat a few random vegetarian things to make up a full meal: bread with cheese, salad, baked potato, etc. Every other night of the year, my family eats microwave dinners. None of us cook. I eat meatless frozen pizza. Hopefully someday we'll have similar schedules—then we could start to cook and eat together."

"I experiment a lot on my family, and lately they've been more supportive of me. Like I made this really nasty tofu stuff and it was awful. It was the first time I ever made anything with tofu, and it just didn't turn out. They were really nice about it. Usually I make my own meals. It will be a frozen veggie burger and or salad or steamed vegetables or something like that, and my family, they just kind of watch me."

"I experiment a lot with food. My family watches me in amazement, wondering why I subject myself to such messes as silken tofu, when I could just eat what Mom makes. Then they watch me eat 'weird' things like tabouli with fresh mint, or falafel, and wonder why I made this turn for the worse called vegetarianism. Sometimes other people tell my parents they think it's great I'm so interested in my health. 'You must be so proud,' they say. After enough comments like that, my parents are starting to believe that vegetarianism is a good thing."

parental concern: where's the protein?

Add these great protein sources to your vegetarian shopping list:

- Legumes such as garbanzo beans, black beans, pinto beans, and split peas.
- Veggie burgers (wheat or soy), such as Boca Burgers or Amy's.
- Tofu, either firm, soft, marinated, or freeze-dried.
- Tempeh (fermented soy beans), either plain or with added rice or veggies.
- Mock duck or chicken (wheat gluten), which is usually marinated and fresh or canned.
- Texturized Vegetable Protein (dried soy flakes), which can be soaked and cooked like ground meat.
- VEAT (soy products), which come as "fish," or "chicken."
- Morningstar Farms (soy products), such as vegetarian bacon, sausage, or chicken patties.

"When I initially stopped eating meat, my mom bought some dehydrated vegetarian mix that claimed to be 'just like ground beef!' when you add water. Wow! It was disgusting. She made me eat it, just to prove that this is what being a vegetarian means. It has taken years for her to realize that you don't have to eat fake meat out of a box to be a vegetarian. There are a million good-tasting ways to eat a well-balanced diet and lots of good sources of protein. Now I don't like to eat anything highly processed or anything made with a mix, and none of my protein comes in a powdered form! There is nothing better for the earth and for my body than fresh food. Three seasons of the year, my city has an outdoor farmers' market. You can find locally grown flowers, produce, and other things people have made for much cheaper than at the grocery store. Eating that way, your diet changes with the seasons."

If I Could Only Say. . .

Obviously, it isn't easy being a vegetarian in a meat-eating home. But you persevere. But, we wondered, how could life be made easier? How could you get your parents over to *your* side, the green side?

Question: *If you could say anything to your parents about your vegetarianism or vegetarianism in general, what would you say?*

Replies:

"'You don't have to buy me *meat*.' It's is the most expensive thing at the grocery store. Don't you want to save some money?"

"'I'm worried about your health.' A vegetarian diet may lower the risk for heart disease, diabetes, obesity, and some cancers. Isn't that reason enough to make the switch?"

"'Please accept my decision as a valid one.' I don't think I'll give vegetarianism up if they give me a hard enough time about it. If they would accept it, we would get along much better."

"My family is Catholic. I know the tenets of our religion to be true, just as I know that it is cruel to slaughter animals for their meat. They need to understand that my conviction runs deep."

"I wish my parents could live a day in the life of an animal. They don't understand the compassion I feel for other living things. I want them to understand that animals have feelings, too. I tried to use words to explain this to my mom, but they went right over her head. Then, I had her watch a video, 'Diet for New America,' by John Robbins. In one scene, a reporter interviewed a dairy farmer who was bottle-feeding a calf. He was asked, 'Do you take the calves away from their mothers right after they're born?' to which the farmer responded, 'No, that would be cruel. We leave them with them for at least twenty-four hours.' That did it—my mom understood and felt compassion for the baby cow because *she* is a mom. Sometimes you have to try a few different approaches before your family understands what you're trying to teach them. Once they get it, though, they won't forget. My mom stopped eating meat after seeing that documentary."

an advocate worth reading

Diet for a New America: How Your Food Choices Affect Your Health, Happiness and the Future of Life on Earth by John Robbins (Stillpoint Publishing,1987) is about "factory farms." Robbins, medical director of the California Institute for Health and Healing, details how livestock are raised under increasingly industrialized conditions. Natural ways of raising animals, including grazing and foraging, have been replaced by inhumane and unhealthy practices, says Robbins. He also debunks nutritional myths perpetuated by the food industries, including his family's Baskin-Robbins ice-cream empire.

"I'd say, 'Don't worry.' My family thinks there is something wrong with you if you choose to be a vegetarian. I want to take them to a vegetarian restaurant, or somewhere else where lots of vegetarians congregate, to show them it isn't a bad, weird thing to do. I'm still the same person I've always been, I just don't eat meat anymore."

"'Thank you.' My parents are really supportive of my vegan diet; my dad is a vegan himself. I want them to know how thankful I am that they are so open-minded and willing to help me in all of my pursuits."

Hear, Hear!

We couldn't help but notice the emotion you displayed when talking about your trials and tribulations in gaining acceptance at home. It's tough to be serious about something and not be taken seriously! What parental reactions, we wondered, upset you the most?

Posting: *Please fill in the blank. It p****s me off when my parents react to my vegetarianism by: _____.*

Fill-ins:

"Insisting that there is nothing wrong with eating meat and that the animals 'don't care.'"

"Cooking meat for dinner every night and refusing to buy Boca Burgers, even when I put them on the grocery list."

"Telling me the Bible condemns vegetarians."

"Making me eat poultry or fish sometimes and telling me to stop being so radical about things."

"Insisting that I fit their standard of perfection, and that vegetarianism isn't part of their ideal."

"Making a sarcastic comments and jokes about it. Telling me it's just a phase, and asking when I'm going to grow out of it."

"Saying that they wish they had been there to protect me when I got abducted by aliens (it was kind of funny at first, though)."

Suggestions for Family Concerns

This teen's list of potential parent problems sums it up well. We've offered some suggestions in italics, but you'll have lots of ideas, too.

The feeling of rejection. They are sad and mad because they feel there will no longer be any of those sentimental Sunday family dinners. *Assure your parents that you will still sit with them at the dinner table. Dinnertime is more than just about eating; it's an important time for kids and their parents to connect.*

Restaurant problems. They'll be cross; they'll feel that you can't go out as a family to dine anymore because there won't be anything for you to eat. *Search out some restaurants that offer food that both the meat eaters and the vegetarians in the family will enjoy! It is not that hard!*

Food choice problems. Grandparents often have a harder time adapting. Parents and grandparents may think that you will still eat chicken or fish and be even more upset when you refuse. *Be clear with your family about what you will and won't eat. Be firm but respectful. Offer to bring a vegetarian dish when you visit relatives.*

Faced with temptation. Your parents may try to tempt you to be "normal" again by waving all the meats "that you always loved so much" under your nose. *Be firm but respectful and ask them to respect your wishes. Remind them that you are not trying to force them to be vegetarian.*

Big meat eaters. If your family are big meat eaters, you may find it even harder than if your family eats meat and fish only moderately. You may also encounter the difficulty of cleanliness in cooking utensils because of cross-contamination. *Learn how to cook and be prepared to wash dishes and cooking utensils!*

Special shopping needs. You may have a problem finding health food stores or brands that cater to vegetarians, and you could encounter the issue of added expense. *Note, however, that meat is also costly. Most large grocery stores carry lots of vegetarian options. You do not need to shop in health food stores.*

Morals and ethics. If you are vegetarian because of animal ethics, your parents or friends might tease you and might start saying things like 'oh you can't sit on that chair, it's leather.' *Take another look at chapters 2 and 3 to see how teens said they responded to these remarks! Experiment until you find the response that works best for you!*

"Bashing it and saying it's unhealthy when they know it's better than eating animal products."

"Sighing and acting 'harmed' and 'stressed' about having to make different things for my diet."

"Saying it's pointless and that I'm not making any difference or saving any animals. Reminding me that I am anemic to start with, and vegetarianism will only make me sicker."

"Saying, 'What are you cooking? It smells gross!'"

"Telling me I'm not getting the nutrients I need in order to grow."

Break It to Them Gently

There is a lot of discussion on the Internet about how to discuss your intentions to become vegetarian with your parents. Most of the advice we found to be very sound. Here are a few basic, good rules from fellow teenagers:

GET THE FACTS RIGHT

"The best thing you can do for yourself as well as for your parents is to educate yourself. Figure out your own nutritional needs, and then research foods to find out what you need to include in your diet. Read about alternate protein sources. Make sure that the calcium you consume can be easily absorbed. Check your iron to make sure you aren't starting out deficient, and then figure out what you have to eat to prevent anemia. Find out how many calories you need every day, and keep a journal for a week to see if you are over or under. This way, when your parents accuse you of making unhealthy choices, you've got the facts to prove otherwise."

BE READY FOR THE DISCUSSION

"Deciding to go vegetarian, or making any other big lifestyle change, is inevitably going to cause some sort of discussion. Whether it is positive or negative depends on your family. You have to be willing to listen to your parents' side of the story. Hopefully, if you listen to them they'll listen to you. But be prepared to encounter some resistance. Show them your choice to go vegetarian is well-thought-out and healthy."

PRESENT FULL MEAL PLANS

"Presenting a full meal plan in your discussion will make it easier for them, especially if they aren't doing a lot of the cooking. Get cookbooks and show them how to adapt family recipes. For example, show them how they can take a favorite recipe that uses ground beef and use veggie meat instead. Also present the health standpoint. For example, tell them, 'I understand that you think that meat is really good because it has protein and iron, but I can get protein and iron from my vegetarian diet, too.'"

TAKING THE FIRST STEP

"If you are on good speaking terms with your parents, then it shouldn't be too difficult to talk to them about it. You need to explain clearly your reasons and ask for their support. Don't let them feel you are rejecting them. Make sure you have done plenty of research so that they can see that you are serious about it, that it's not just a passing phase and that you will be sensible. Having documents on hand about nutrition can also help when they object about the 'health risks' of being vegetarian or vegan."

Summing It Up

Parents respond to teen vegetarianism in a variety of ways. Some parents are very supportive. Some even become vegetarian themselves. Others are totally against vegetarianism and make it very difficult to be meat-free without a continual battle. Most parents are somewhere in between. It is helpful to:

- have plenty of *accurate* facts, especially about nutrition, as this is a primary worry of parents. Chapter 8 offers plenty.

- develop the skills needed to be a vegetarian. These skills include menu planning, shopping, and food preparation. Sharing new foods is a great way to get your parents and family interested in your vegetarianism.

living in a
nonvegetarian world

TEENAGERS ARE SOCIAL CREATURES. THEY PAL AROUND WITH LOTS OF FRIENDS IN A VARIETY OF SOCIAL VENUES. FOOD IS A BIG PART OF IT ALL. SO IS PEER PRESSURE.

IT'S LIKELY THAT ONE OF THE REASONS YOU BECAME A VEGETARIAN IS BECAUSE YOUR VIEW OF THE MEAT-EATING WORLD CHANGED. WILL THIS AFFECT YOUR RELATIONSHIP WITH YOUR MEAT-EATING FRIENDS? MORE TO THE POINT, WILL THEY ACCEPT THE CHANGE IN *YOU?*

If your friends are supportive of your choice, that's great. But it's not always the case. When you go out with friends or out on a date, you may become the odd person out when deciding where to dine and what to eat. You may feel that you must constantly defend your decision to eat something different. Stereotyping of vegetarians could even cause you some awkward moments if a prying peer teases you about your changed lifestyle.

How have other teens handled some of these situations? Very well, we are happy to say. Becoming a vegetarian doesn't mean you have to give up your meat-eating friends—unless, of course, you want to.

Friends or Friends Alike?

The first thing we wanted to find out is if vegetarian teens hung out together. Does turning vegetarian cost you your meat-eating friends? Do you gradually stray away from the old gang? Or maybe it just doesn't matter. To find out if vegetarian and meat-eating teens mix well together, we asked the following question.

Question: *Are many of your friends vegetarian?*

Replies:

"Yes, like me, many philosophy majors or people who are into ethics are vegetarian. Also, I am involved in student groups like SOAR (Student Organization for Animal Rights) and CAA (Compassionate Action for Animals), and my friends in these groups are vegetarian. I tend to respect people more who are vegetarian. I actually seek out friends who are vegetarian. My friends are all aware that I am vegan— I am proud of my veganism."

"Unfortunately, not many of my friends are vegetarian. But now that I've been working with the student organization for animal rights, I've met a lot of people who are veg. Also, protesting is a way to meet other vegetarians. But, I'd say maybe 10 to 20 percent of my friends are vegetarian or vegan. And I've actually converted a lot of my friends who were die-hard meat eaters. A couple actually went vegan."

"Actually, none of my friends are vegetarian. My roommate eats chicken, fish, and the occasional hamburger. My boyfriend is the extreme opposite; he is the definition of carnivorous. I also work at a vegetarian *un*-friendly restaurant. In other words, I don't spend much time in places where I could meet other vegetarians. I end up adapting to the carnivores around me, for example by cooking vegetables for all of

86

us and chicken they can add separately. I don't mind handling and cooking meat, I just choose not to eat it."

"Some of my friends are vegetarian. Earlier, when I was in middle school and high school, nobody was. They all thought I was a little crazy. Since then, I have moved progressively toward activist circles, where a lot of people are vegetarian."

"A lot of my friends around here are 'vegetarian sympathizers.' They eat vegetarian most of the time and seem to believe in the philosophy of vegetarianism, but still eat meat when it's offered. They don't want to make a commitment; they don't want to swear off meat; they want room for flexibility in their diets. They don't think strict vegetarianism is important."

"I don't have any vegetarian friends, which means that people harass me all the time about my eating habits. No one understands why I've made this choice, and they all think I'm weird. I have to read books and visit chat rooms to remind myself that I'm not the only vegetarian in the world."

"I have two vegetarian friends. The rest of my friends make a joke out of it, but they have gradually gotten used to it. They understand that I'll take care of my own food when we eat together. One of my friend's families makes a full vegetarian meal every time I eat over, and makes everyone eat *my* way for once. That's cool!"

"One of my friends is particularly skeptical. She said, 'I couldn't become a vegetarian. It wouldn't go over very well living in a farming community. Besides, vegetarian diets are unhealthy. You can't get enough iron—you need to eat meat for that. If you lived in my community you'd understand.' She reminds me that our views on diet and lifestyle are directly related to the values of the community in which we live. Vegetarianism is unheard of in her community, because meat is their livelihood. I do my best to help her understand there are more ways to do things than what you grew up with."

"More of my friends were vegetarian when it was trendy within the liberal community. Now, with meat eating in style, many people are back on the bandwagon, believing that meat is the best source of protein and a quick way to lose weight."

Different Strokes

No doubt the majority of your friends are nonvegetarian, too. What kind of reaction can you expect when you make this change, which they likely will view as drastic?

Question: *How do your friends react to your being or becoming vegetarian?*

Replies:

"A lot of them say, 'It's okay if that's what you want to do, just don't push it on me.' I feel so strongly about the animal rights issue that it comes up a lot. Some of my friends have started to mock me; they don't care what I have to say. They bring up some weird 'fact' about vegetarians and then don't listen when I defend my position. But then, for every close-minded person I know there is someone who pays attention to what I have to say."

"It's such a hard topic to talk about because people are generally against animal cruelty, but actually making the switch to vegetarian is so difficult. It is hard to change a lifestyle that you've been living for all these years. That's why I think it's such a hostile topic. Some will say 'Stop lecturing me!' and it's ironic, because they are the ones who started the discussion. After I tell them the reality of how animal products are made, they don't want to listen. Then they accuse me of preaching."

"I don't know why they're my friends, but every time we eat together they ask, 'Do you want some of this?' Like shoving meat at me or doing really stupid stuff like that. Or 'Wow, look! A piece of meat in your food!' One of my friends used to ask me 'what if?' questions all the time. Like, 'What if you were stranded on a desert island and there was nobody else there but a cow? Would you eat the cow? Well, what if the cow just died, what if you just found the cow lying dead—would you eat it then?' I said, 'Would you eat a piece of meat that you just found on the ground?'"

"I realize that their opinion doesn't matter and they eat what they want to eat and I eat what I want to eat. Whether it's related to being vegetarian or not, I think that that's the way it should be anyway—as long as you're taking good care of yourself. I've noticed that a lot of nonvegetarian people are very interested in vegan cooking, because it's fun to learn about new foods. If you're eliminating meat, you are forced to look for other sources of protein, such as beans, lentils, and nuts. For a lot of people, celebrating with food means overeating or cooking the same things you've been cooking for the last ten years. Vegetarian or veganism is a healthy way to celebrate with food and make cooking fun."

"I think people look down and say that animals don't count—they don't matter. I'm a Christian and my friends say that God gave us animals so we could eat them. I don't even bring up religion as a reason I'm vegetarian. I think there's a lot more logic behind the other issues that you can prove, for example, that there's so much grain being consumed by cows that could feed humans. For me, it is easier to talk about feeding more people with grains than what God intends for us to eat."

the bible's meat-eating policy

Does the Bible espouse, deplore, or ignore eating meat as a natural part of human existence? It is a controversial subject that depends on the way in which the Bible is interpreted.

Some biblical scholars suggest that the biblical references to eating meat or flesh reflect a translation issue where "meat" really means "food." Take, for example, the parable of Jesus serving a crowd with "loaves and fishes." Some scholars believe that Jesus wasn't feeding the crowd fish but, rather, fish rolls made from a marine plant that was commonly eaten in Babylonian times. Others suggest that the fish in the story was symbolic; fish was a symbol used by early Christians.

Not only do some passages in the Bible talk about eating only plants, others refer to all animals having a soul. Take a look at this verse from Genesis 1:30: "And to every beast on the earth, and to every fowl of the air, and to everything that creepeth upon the earth, everything that has the breath of life, I have given every green herb for food." For more information on religion and vegetarianism, read *Diet for Transcendence* by Steven Rosen.

"My friends' reactions are kind of mixed. I'd say half of them love it. I have one friend who would be vegetarian, but he eats meat some of the time. He's a vegetarian waiting to come out of the closet! He and I have fun cooking together. I have three or four friends that are vegetarians, period. Otherwise, my other friends poke fun at me for being vegetarian. Like when I'm at the lunch table and they're all sitting there eating hamburgers and I'm eating a salad, they call me a 'strange hippy,' 'country hair,' or something like that. It doesn't really bother me."

"When I first started, my friends thought I was just trying to be cool, like, 'Oh, I'm a vegetarian.' They thought I was being a dork until they realized the reason I was doing it. This is just me, it's what I want to do."

"When I first became a vegetarian, I was in junior high. I got so much crap for it. I felt on the defensive all the time. But now as people are realizing that I've been vegetarian for five years and it doesn't look like I'm going to stop, they're pretty respectful of it. Sometimes, I have sleepovers with my hockey friends, and in the morning the parents make pancakes and sausage. Once the sausage plate was sitting right next to me and one of my friends saw it and said, 'Oh my gosh, I can't believe that just happened to you.' I said 'What?' 'The sausage was sitting right next to you, doesn't that bother you?' And I said 'Not really, I don't care.' So, it's really cool that all my friends are always making sure that if we go somewhere, I will be able to find something to eat. It's usually not a problem at all. And my parents are really cool about it now, too."

"People have a really strong bias against those who feel compassion for, and protest in favor of, animal rights. My idea of what veganism is has evolved and gotten a lot more complex since I first started, but at the root of it is still that sense I get when I think of an animal being hurt. I think people who are vegans for environmental reasons win more respect from the general public than those who are vegan for animal rights issues. That may be because animal rights activists tend to be louder in their protesting, and more antiestablishment."

vegetarian breakfast treats

Breakfast foods are the latest trend from veggie burger producers. Try Boca meatless sausage patties and links, Morningstar Farm's meatless bacon, sausage patties, and sausage links. Gardenburger also offers meatless breakfast sausage. They are all low in fat, but like most soy products, are a bit pricey.

Out and About Food Places

Eating out and sharing are part of American culture. Chain restaurants where chicken wings and meat-filled nachos are offered are popular choices. How do you affect the scene? To find out, we asked the following:

Question: *When you're going out with your friends, how do they (or you) generally handle the fact that you're vegetarian?*

Replies:

"The more vegetarians or vegans in the group, the easier it is to choose a restaurant with veg options. When I'm the only one, I get stuck at a hamburger place, eating the bun and the lettuce."

"My friends are the best. They always let me choose where we go, to insure that I have options. Most restaurants are very accommodating. You can always get pasta without meat or chicken on it. As long as you're comfortable asking the server to make sure your meal is meat-free, vegetarians can eat almost anywhere."

"At my friend's cabin this summer, we went to either Taco Bell, Burger King, or McDonald's every day. Finally, I convinced her to try Subway. That's where I have the most choices."

"At restaurants, I usually ask about ingredients. Even with bread. For example, I'll ask, 'Can you check the label on your bread—does it have any milk in it?' That was really hard to get used to. I had one vegan friend who used to do that and I thought, 'You're crazy! You can't possibly ask them to read all the labels!' But people are pretty cool about it actually. I've had cooks bring their jug of oil or grease to my table. They'll say, 'See—read it for yourself, there's no dairy in it.'"

what's a nice vegetarian like you doing in a place like this?

Can you still hang out at fast-food restaurants with your meat-eating buddies? The answer is, yes, but your choices of what to eat will be limited. Here is what we found out about some of the popular fast-food joints.

Subway is a great choice for vegetarians. You can design your sandwich to be meat and/or dairy free. Some branches even offer a soy turkey sub or other meat substitute.

Taco Bell is another good choice for vegetarians because nearly all of their dishes can be prepared with or without meat. They also offer a few strictly vegetarian options, like the Bean Tostada, Veggie Fajita Wrap, and Breakfast Quesadilla.

McDonald's offers Granola Shakes, Butter Biscuits, McDonaldland cookies, and a McSalad Shaker. Watch out for the French fries; they have beef flavoring. Check out www.mcdonalds.com for ingredients and nutrient information.

Burger King, on the other hand, isn't so great; the veggie burgers are cooked in the same oil as the meat. Burger King even manages to smuggle non-dairy animal products (like lard!) into their milk shakes. The only safe bet is the basic salad.

"I'm to the point now, when people ask me questions, that I ask them if they are really interested or if they are just trying to egg me on. Some people are really rude. But the people who are genuinely interested, I'm happy to explain to them anything that they want to know. Most people are interested in why I don't eat honey." [For an explanation as to why some vegetarians don't eat honey, see page 27.]

the vegetarian challenge

Fuddrucker's and Red Lobster didn't design their menus with vegetarians in mind. At Fuddrucker's, your only choices are the garden burger, Idaho baked potato, Caesar salad, or dinner salad. At Red Lobster, hope that they'll let you order a salad or pasta entrée without the meat or the fish, because nothing on their menu is vegetarian. We couldn't even find a garden salad!

"Seafood places are hard for me, because so many things on the menu are *just* fish. If I asked them to leave the fish out, there wouldn't be anything left but the lemon wedge. I usually hope to find a pasta dish, so that I can order plain noodles. Also, a guy once took me on a date to Fuddrucker's. I should have told him I was vegetarian before he picked me up."

"I almost always find vegetarian appetizers at restaurants. Then, if nothing else, I can eat two or three of those for dinner."

best bets for eating out as a teen vegetarian

For a great list of vegetarian-friendly restaurant chains, check out www.vegetarian-restaurants.net. Some choices include Applebee's, Chili's, Olive Garden, and Chipotle. Check out the Vegetarian Plate at Applebee's, which offers steamed broccoli, cauliflower, zucchini, and potatoes. At Chili's try the tortilla with beans and a garden salad. Olive Garden is a bit more challenging but, if it is a family favorite, you'll be safe with the breadsticks and marina sauce. Both are vegan. If you don't eat eggs, you'll need to stay away from the Eggplant Parmigiana, which has eggs in the breading. Chipotle allows you to create your own meatless burritos with beans, rice, and veggies.

"A lot of my friends worry if I can only eat a salad. I explain that it's okay, I'll make up for it later. I'll eat more when I get home. I go out with my friends to have a good time and to hang out with them. Eating a big meal is not my first priority."

Would You Like to Stay for Dinner?

Going over to someone's house for a meal can be particularly touchy, since friends or their parents are the ones providing the food. What do you do in a nonvegetarian situation without being rude?

Question: *If you were to go over to a friend's house for dinner, would most of your friends know you're vegetarian? Would they tell their parents or do you just handle it when you get there?*

Replies:

"There have been a couple of times when my friends forgot to tell their parents that I'm vegetarian. When that happens, I eat around the meat as inconspicuously as possible. My friends always notice, though, and apologize. They feel horrible for putting me in such an awkward position."

"Generally people know and we all cook together. It's rarely a problem anyway, because so many of my friends are vegetarian. I almost always make a point to bring something to share that is vegan, too."

"I had one experience when I was asked to stay for dinner at my friend's house. Her parents asked, 'Do you want chicken legs, or do you want pork chops?' I finally said, 'Actually, I'm a vegetarian,' and they're like, 'What are you a vegetarian for? You're going to die when you're twenty-six.' They kept going. I was so annoyed with them, and my friend didn't say anything to support me. I felt like I was a 'princess' and people had to cater to me. I don't want to feel like that. So that's my least favorite thing about being a vegetarian. I can find my own options. I don't need people to go out of their way for me."

"Going over to other people's houses is harder than eating out. Once, I went over to my aunt and uncle's house for Thanksgiving and they said, 'I found you this really healthy bread, it's vegan.' After reading the list of ingredients I found out it had honey in it. So I just didn't eat it. They asked me why not, and I said, 'It's not really vegan, I'm sorry.' I feel bad because people really try a lot of the time. But usually when

I know I'm going over to someone's to eat, then I say, 'You know I'm a vegan, can you possibly make something for me or make sure you have something available that I can eat?' Or when I go to a family's house I bring my own little tub of margarine."

looking for vegetarian margarine

If you are a lacto-vegetarian, finding butter and margarine that you can eat shouldn't be a problem. Butter is made from milk fat, and most margarines are made from vegetable oils. Some margarines, however, include some milk products (like whey) in their ingredient listings. If you want a dairy-free margarine, try the Earth Balance brand.

"I always tell people I'm a vegan, but that they don't have to make anything special. I don't want my hosts to stress out over me; I'm perfectly happy with salad. Plus, people often try to be really helpful by buying me veggie burgers, only to find out they contain lactose. I feel the worst if they've gone out of their way specifically for me, and then I have to tell them I can't eat it. I am always as polite as possible about it, though. I make sure to thank them, sincerely, for trying to accommodate me."

meatless burgers are not created equal

You'll need to check the label to see if your favorite veggie burger is vegan, because many commercial veggie burgers include dairy and egg products. Here is what we found out:

Boca offers six different meatless burgers. The All-American and four other "flavors" are safe for lacto-ovo vegetarians as most contain cheese. The Original-Vegan is—you guessed it—vegan.

Gardenburger offers two vegan options: the Flame Grilled Burger and the Garden Vegan Burger. Other Gardenburger varieties contain milk products.

Morningstar Farms has nine meatless burgers. Check the list of ingredients to see which are safe for you.

"I get nervous every time a friend asks me to stay for dinner. When they find out I'm vegetarian, they offer to make me something special. I hate that because of how guilty it makes me feel. It's much easier to eat out at a restaurant, where you have some control over what you eat. For example, the other night for the fourth of July my mom and one of my best friends from high school and I went out to eat. My mom and my friend really wanted to go to a sit-down-meal place and the only place that was really available was a steakhouse. I thought, 'Oh great!' But at the same time, I didn't want them to miss out on something, so I said, 'Yeah, sure, let's go,' and I searched the menu. That's the thing—if you go somewhere and you're with new friends, just take a look at the menu before you actually decide to go there. Then find something you can eat. I ended up having a salad and some appetizers."

"My parents decided not to tell my relatives that I'm vegetarian, which means I have to do it myself. Nobody believes me unless I am very assertive. You can't sit back and pick around the meat, you have to say 'No, I'm not going to have that!' My grandparents have gotten quite mad at me. I remember one time last Christmas, I was sitting next to my grandma and when the turkey came around, she took some of it and put it on my plate. I said, 'No grandma, I'm not going to eat this,' and she just grabbed more and put it onto my plate. You have to be assertive about it and say, 'I'm not going to do this.' You have to find a way to get the point across, while remaining tolerant and respectful."

"Say I get invited to a friend's house or a prospective girlfriend's family that doesn't know I'm a vegetarian yet. I just find it better that you let them know it up-front. Because if you try to hide it and then they question you on it, they feel bad that you didn't say something. A lot of people are understanding. One or two members of my family now have something different prepared for me when I come to visit. I love that. I don't require it or ask them to do that, but those are the aunts and uncles who truly understand and truly like to help me."

"Generally, I don't say too much because I don't want it to be an issue. I don't like it when my vegetarianism makes life harder for the people around me. I want it to be something that is really easy, positive, and potentially influential. Nobody around me will think about going vegetarian if they see it producing awkward, unpleasant situations. One time I went over to my boyfriend's house and met his mom for the first time. She made chicken–wild rice soup, and I did my best to eat around the chicken. But that's probably the only time that I've really felt awkward. Now I'd probably say something because I'm not that passive, and because my boyfriend and I have been dating for a while."

Just You and Mr. Beef

How flexible or strict are you willing to be when it comes to communal eating with nonvegetarian friends? Is there a situation in which vegetarians are willing to eat meat?

Question: *Is it okay for vegetarians to cook meat for their friends? Describe a situation in which you might eat meat.*

Replies:

"I don't think it's okay to cook meat for others, because you're still supporting the killing of the animal by facilitating its consumption. If someone around you is cooking or eating meat, you have to be respectful of their choices. The only time (only, only, only time) I'd eat meat is if I needed it to survive—if I were on a desert island and there were no plants or anything—just me and a hamburger. I'm eating the hamburger."

"I wouldn't say that cooking meat for your friends is bad. I mean, if we expect them to provide vegetarian food for us when we go to their house, then it would only be polite to provide them with the same. I wouldn't though. Being a vegan, for me, is protesting against the horrible mistreatment of factory farm animals. By buying meat or animal products, I feel that I am contributing to their suffering and meaningless death. If I were to have friends over for dinner, then I would not cook them tofu or anything that might seem strange to them. I would probably cook them pasta or something else more familiar, so we could all be happy. I think the only situation in which I would ever even consider eating meat would be life or death. If I was stranded in the middle of nowhere and would die unless I killed an animal and ate it, I would do it."

"No! I wouldn't cook them something really weird, but I wouldn't cook them meat. The way I see it, they can eat vegetarian food, but we can't eat their food. I hate when people say, 'I'm not a vegetarian, so I'm not gonna eat vegetables.' Okay, they usually don't say those exact words but something along those lines. I would never ever, ever, eat meat."

"I personally wouldn't cook meat. I stand up against meat, and if my friends really want to eat some, they can cook it themselves. I would never eat meat; I wouldn't kill several lives for my own."

"I would say, 'No'. I wouldn't touch meat because of the bad karma attached to it. I want no part of suffering or cruelty inflicted on another being. As long as I have control over a situation, I'll do my best to avoid harming others. If that control were taken away from me, for example, if I were comatose and being tube fed, I really would have no choice. If I were ever in jail for any reason, I might resort to eating dairy or eggs if my health absolutely depended on it for lack of vegan foods. But in no way would I eat meat."

Karma is a term from eastern philosophy. It is sometimes equated with "fate" but also has a deeper meaning drawing from a belief in reincarnation. Karma is the force or influence that one's past life has on one's current life, with every action on earth creating good or bad karma. You also create karma in your daily life; what you do, say, and think today directly affects your tomorrow. If you choose a compassionate, vegetarian diet, for example, you will be rewarded with compassion. Some believe that consuming a slaughtered cow is bad karma because the animal was frightened just before it was killed, one might ingest its fear and unhappiness.

"I personally would not cook meat for friends. Real friends would understand why. I would never change my beliefs because of being in another country and never at someone's house. Ever."

Expect: Disbelief, Anger, Curiosity

Many of our interviewees had great advice about dealing with nonvegetarians. The following response is smart, to the point, and sums it up very well.

"Friends and acquaintances generally have three reactions to the statement 'I'm a vegetarian': disbelief, anger, and curiosity. The disbelievers question you. They ask, 'Do you really eat no chicken?' and 'Don't you cheat?' (as if being vegetarian was a weight-loss program). These types of disbelievers generally are no worse than well-meaning fools. You should explain to them the what, why, and how if they ask—otherwise, answer quickly and move on. The ones that are angry and condemn you for being vegetarian will attack. They want to challenge you by saying, 'You can't be healthy. You can't be fine.' And my favorite: 'Humans were meant to eat meat.' Sometimes I bite my tongue to keep from saying, 'And we were meant to die from heart disease and obesity, too, I guess.' You should *not*, I repeat, *not* try to win an argument unless they say something obviously stupid. Most of these people will not change their minds, as they honestly believe they are right. That's okay. You know you're right, too. For the genuinely curious, talk to them and explain. Answer their questions; recommend books, websites, and articles. Lend them materials. They might be your first converts. And if they decide being veggie is not for them, don't pressure them. At least you tried. Oh, and one other thing. It is not necessary to shout at the world explaining you are vegetarian. I went to a camp for an entire week, and brought, cooked, and ate my own food. Three people asked about it. Most people will not care unless you make a stink out of it. Tell whom you must. Everyone else can figure it out. Some people may view the approach I advocate as too lax, too casual, and not likely to help. However, from what I have seen, leading by example works. If you are not afraid to ask for a meatless meal, maybe the person behind you will see what you are doing and recognize it as valuable. Maybe they will be bold next time and ask for 'everything but the meat.' Honestly, you never know. But it might work, and remember—you *will* survive your meat-eating encounters."

The Dating Game

Can being vegetarian interfere with relationships among couples in which one partner is not a believer? It seems to depend on how serious the relationship is.

Question: *Would you ever choose to date someone who wasn't vegetarian or vegan?*

Replies:

"I really couldn't see it in a very strong relationship because being vegan is such a fundamental belief. I had the experience of dating someone who was just vegetarian, and even then there was this really significant issue of our differences. It felt like I always had to make special demands when we went out to eat. It's different with other friends, or the people you only see once in a while. With significant others, they end up having to make so many sacrifices in order to accommodate their vegan counterparts. Eventually, they may start to resent you for your 'rigid' lifestyle. In other words, I've found it's easier in the long run to date another vegan. And I could never raise kids with someone who wasn't vegan. It would be too hard."

"I wouldn't just date vegetarians. In fact, the boy I'm beginning to get involved with eats meat and lots of it. I think that being a vegetarian is a personal opinion and decision. I have no right to discriminate against other people or press my beliefs on them."

"When I begin to look for a life partner, their beliefs about food, the environment, and animal rights will be very important. But for now, as long as I like them and they like me and they respect my vegan beliefs, then fine."

"If I truly love someone, I don't think I'll care if they eat meat or not. Diet choices are such a small part of a person's entire being. The problem is, I don't want to buy meat or other animal products. Maybe we'll have to go grocery shopping individually."

"I don't have a problem dating meateaters. Vegetarianism is a personal choice, and just because somebody doesn't have the compassion I do for animals doesn't mean that they are undateable."

"I wouldn't date a carnivore because I can't imagine kissing one. I don't want to put my lips where animal flesh has gone! Actually, if the boy really liked me, this would be a huge incentive for him to convert!"

"He-Man Eat Meat" Thinking

Not only are more vegetarians female, we also discovered that overall males are less likely to accept vegetarianism than are females. Why, we wondered, are meat-eating guys so tough about it? To find out, we asked the following:

Question: *Why do you think that young guys are more reluctant to understand or are less curious about vegetarianism than young women?*

Replies:

"Boys don't think vegetarianism is an appropriately masculine choice. It's like, 'Oh, that's a girl thing.' It has become a gender issue—boys gotta eat meat, you gotta be tough. But what does eating meat have to do with being tough?"

more and more male vegetarians

Today's male teenagers appear to be more open to vegetarianism than previous generations. Our research suggests that approximately 4 to19 percent of adult vegetarians are male. In our study of vegetarian teens, we found that about 26 percent of teen vegetarians are male.

"When I first became vegan, there was only one male vegan at our school. He was teased every day about it. I'm sure he was teased more for his choice of diet than he would have been for a certain religion or skin color. I always wondered why veganism was such a target. I've since come to understand that veganism in males is often associated with homo- or bisexuality, and that elicits a lot of teasing. Vegans and homosexuals share some common stereotypes, like femininity, social consciousness, and frailty."

"A lot of guys think it's manly to consume meat. You know, 'I work out and I eat meat to help build my muscles.' And vegetarianism is something compassionate, even if you are doing it purely for your own health. It still comes down to making the decision that you are not killing animals, which is a compassionate decision, and being more compassionate and nurturing are typically feminine qualities."

"As a boy, I find I have to explain my vegetarianism more often than I would if I were a girl. People expect it from girls, or at least know how to react because they've seen it in so many others. Us boys get asked a ton more questions."

Political Awareness

Since vegetarianism is considered extremist to so many "outsiders," we've found that people associate vegetarianism with liberalism or being politically to the left. Today's vegetarian teens, however, are taking the view that they are more politically aware in general, and not necessarily more leftist.

Question: *Do you think vegetarianism has to do with a political affiliation?*

Postings:

"Vegetarianism is more than a meat-free diet, it's a statement. A Nobel Laureate, Isaac Singer, claimed that vegetarianism was his statement, 'and it is a strong one.' With more and more adolescents adopting meat-free lifestyles, vegetarianism has become a means of rebellion. It's a rebellion against world hunger and poverty; it's a rebellion against poor health. But most of all, vegetarianism should be a rebellion against cruelty."

"Most teenage vegetarians aren't necessarily politically active but are more into discussions regarding current affairs and issues. Some, of course, don't know anything about politics and have no well-informed opinions on government."

Bad Stereotyping!

Speaking of stereotyping, we picked up a lot of buzz on websites about characterizing vegetarianism as compassionate and feminine. Do you feel an alternative lifestyle is a natural extension of these traits?

Question: *Do you think more vegetarians are gay, lesbian, or bisexual than in the general population?*

Replies:

"I think anyone who sees a connection between sexuality and vegetarian or vegan food choices is extremely naïve."

"I think vegetarians have a higher likelihood of 'thinking outside the box' than people who eat a 'regular' American diet. If this means they are more open to non-traditional expressions of sexuality, they may be more likely to come out of the closet."

"Being gay or lesbian or anything else isn't something you can choose, and vegetarianism you do choose. The two don't relate."

"I'd say it's about even. I have gay vegetarian friends and gay non-vegetarian friends. I have straight vegetarian friends and straight non-vegetarian friends. I just happen to be gay and vegetarian but I haven't noticed that there are hoards of us."

a stupid notion

There is no scientific link between vegetarianism and homosexuality. Connections between the two are based purely on stereotypes and should not be perpetuated.

Religion's Influence

Religion and spiritual beliefs are often associated with food habits and other lifestyle choices. For example, many Jewish people eat only kosher foods and Hindus do not eat beef. We wanted to find out if religion was an influence on your decision to become vegetarian.

Question: *Do your religious beliefs have any influence on your being vegetarian? How does your religion view vegetarianism?*

Replies:

"I don't really have an established religion—more like a personal set of beliefs. They directly influenced my decision to become vegetarian. Beliefs like: everyone and everything has a right to live, no one has a right to kill, etc."

"My religion doesn't exist; I don't believe in organized religion. I rejected my Christianity last Christmas Eve after church. In my opinion, organized religion causes more evil and suffering in the world than it does good. Vegetarianism does fit, though, with my own mystical beliefs."

"I am a pastor's daughter. That's right, a P.K. (preacher's kid), so religion is always a big part of my life. When I decided to become a vegan, a lot of people in the congregation looked at me differently. My father showed me different passages from the Bible that say 'it's all right to eat meat' and that God even commanded us to eat meat after the Great Flood. But, I believe that we all have a certain responsibility to the animals of this world. In the beginning, God told Adam and Eve that they were now in charge of the Earth and all the animals that inhabited it. That could be interpreted either as our responsibility to take care of the animals or as permission to use the animals to our benefit. Yes, God may have told us to eat meat, but I doubt he meant for us to do it in this sort of way. Torturing animals and making their lives miserable is definitely not what a loving God had in mind."

"I'm a Christian. Though my beliefs haven't affected my becoming vegetarian (I did that out of my love for all animals), many in my religion think that it's wrong not to eat meat. However, many also believe that Jesus himself would be a vegetarian if he were alive today."

"Being Buddhist, I see no conflict between my religion and my diet. Buddhism is very big on not harming others, and I think a vegetarian lifestyle goes hand in hand with that."

Summing It Up

- Most vegetarians have some friends who are also vegetarian but many who aren't, so social events may require a new set of skills.

- Be up-front about what you do and don't eat in social situations. Offer to bring foods or order independently to make it easier for everyone.

- Many of you said you would date nonvegetarians but that it would be difficult to be with a nonvegetarian in a long-term relationship.

- Most of you saw no relationship between being vegetarian and being gay or lesbian.

- Your personal belief systems support your vegetarianism.

keeping your weight *on!*

N THIS TIME OF EPIDEMIC OBESITY PROBLEMS, WE ARE CON-

CERNED THAT SOME OF YOU COULD VIEW VEGETARIANISM

AS THE ANSWER TO YOUR WEIGHT PROBLEMS. THIS CONCERN

COMES OUT OF OUR PRIOR RESEARCH THAT FOUND VEGETARI-

AN TEENS REPORTED A GREATER NUMBER OF WEIGHT-RELATED

CONCERNS THAN DID NONVEGETARIANS.

In previous research, teen vegetarians were found to be much more likely than nonvegetarians to practice healthy weight-control practices, such as exercising and eating more fruits and vegetables. But on the flip side, they were also more involved in unhealthy weight-control practices, such as laxative use and fasting, than nonvegetarians.

We felt we should explore this area of health and weight management further and find out if data from our survey matched with the experiences of those of you we interviewed for this book. We asked a number of questions that we felt were related to health and weight control, including some about the process of becoming a vegetarian, whether weight loss was the prime motive for the change, whether keeping weight on or off was a major concern of teen vegetarians, and how they made sure they were maintaining a healthy diet. We feel the experiences of these teens will be very helpful to others of you who think about the health and weight implications of your diet.

Slow Starting

Question: *When you decided to become vegetarian, did you do it in one day or was it a process?*

Responses:

"I tried to go vegetarian last year, but I couldn't control my cravings for meat. My mom didn't help matters; she wouldn't stop buying it and cooking it for me. Later, my sister stopped eating meat. She made the switch a lot easier for me, by showing me that there are a lot of really good vegetarian foods. Gradually, I stopped altogether."

"I didn't know a thing about health when I became a vegetarian. stopped eating meat and started eating a ton of dairy products. The when I switched to veganism, I filled up on bread. I didn't realize th meat and dairy I was cutting out of my diet had to be replaced wi other nutritious sources of protein, vitamin, and minerals. Now I e, more nuts, beans, and even tofu. Honestly, before I knew about nut tion, I didn't have any energy. With a balanced diet of fresh foo whole grains, and vegetarian protein sources, I feel awesome expanded my interest in other foods. I eat tofu if it's in Chinese fo but I don't like it any other way. I also started drinking soy milk i place of regular milk. I don't eat fake meat, because I hate the tast of meat and don't like to be reminded of it."

"I ate dairy the whole time I lived with my parents. When I moved ou I became a vegan. Because I can control what foods I buy, I keep animal products that are tempting to me out of the house. I started out simply, substituting cereal and pasta for all the calories I cut out of my diet. Since then, I've been trying to be more and more creative with substitutes. I've tried cooking tofu a million different ways. I really like Japanese noodles with tempeh."

"When I became vegetarian, I increased my intake of whole grains a lot. I also eat a lot of MorningFarms soy meat substitutes for protein."

"Before I knew about alternate protein sources, I lost a lot of weight on the vegetarian diet. Removing meat from my meals meant eating a lot less in general. Then, I started having protein shakes, veggie burgers, and textured vegetable protein. Also, I started eating a lot of salads. Now I eat at least one head of romaine lettuce a day. I'm back to a healthy weight, and I feel better than ever before."

Health Versus Healthy Eating

Question: *How do you make sure that you are eating a healthy diet?*

Responses:

"I had a nutrition unit in my family and consumer science class at school. We talked about the food guide pyramid, and the teacher gave tips on fitting all the essentials into your diet. At first, I kept track of what I ate during the day by putting check marks under columns labeled with each food group. Now that I've gotten accustomed to my healthy diet, I keep an ongoing mental record. Also, my doctor knows that I'm a vegetarian, so whenever I see her she asks me how it's going."

"I do my best to eat a variety of foods. I eat fortified cereals and take a daily multivitamin in order to make sure I'm getting all the vitamins and minerals my body needs. I've been to a nutritionist, so I know there are certain vitamins I have to watch out for, like B_{12}—vitamins that vegetarians can have a hard time fitting into their diets. I know that I should have my bone density checked, too. My mom is worried that I don't get enough calcium as a vegetarian. I cut way back on my milk and cheese when I went vegetarian. She is also worried that I drink too many soft drinks. I think she worries too much!"

bone density and calcium

Calcium is important to teenagers because adolescence is a crucial time for the development of healthy bones. About one-half of adult bone mass is deposited during the teenage years. Inadequate calcium intake during adolescence can increase your chance of having brittle bones later in life, especially if you are female. You need about 1,300 milligrams of calcium every day.

If you substitute soft drinks for drinking milk or fortified soymilk, you may be hurting your bones in two ways. First, you may not be consuming adequate amounts of calcium and secondly, the carbonation and phosphoric acid in soft drinks may actually make it harder for your body to absorb the calcium you do eat.

Bottom line: Make sure that you are getting enough calcium through dairy products or calcium-fortified products (like orange juice). Cut back or eliminate soft drinks altogether.

vitamin supplements on a vegetarian diet

For vegetarians, taking a multivitamin supplement is probably a good idea. Even if you are lacto-ovo, a multivitamin supplement that contains iron, zinc, magnesium, and calcium won't hurt you and might add some protection in case you don't always eat a complete and balanced vegetarian diet.

If your exposure to sunlight is limited or your intake of vitamin D–enriched foods is low, a vitamin D supplement is also recommended. (Note that too much vitamin D is toxic, so you shouldn't take more than 5 micrograms of vitamin D daily.) Some food sources of Vitamin D include Vitamin D-fortified cow's milk, soy milk, margarines and fortified grains. If you are vegan, a supplement that contains vitamin B_{12} is a good idea since B_{12} is difficult to obtain in nonanimal sources.

Keep in mind that a vitamin supplement won't give you *everything* that you need to be healthy. Vitamins provide no energy, and there are important elements that can only be obtained by eating a variety of foods. We believe that there are important, healthful elements in foods that scientists haven't yet identified, so there is no way there could be a supplement for all foods.

Also, avoid taking high levels of any one nutrient. Contrary to claims, excessive amounts of any one nutrient can't make you "super healthy" and may actually be harmful.

"I use a computer program to review my diet and determine what vitamins to take. It is time-consuming, but it shows me where I'm deficient. I also use books."

analyzing your diet

We checked out some online nutrient analysis packages. Some helpful nutrient analysis sites we found include: fitday.com (a free, online fitness journal), foodcount.com (dietary data on 30,000 foods), dietsite.com (weight, exercise, and health tracking), and cookinglight.com (menus and cooking guides). We recommend this website from the Canadian Dietetic Association: www.dietitians.ca/english/frames.html. It is free and fairly easy to use.

"At first I went by how I felt. For example, if I was tired during the day, I added more protein to my meals. I still try and listen to my body, but every six months or so I go on the Internet and relearn how much calcium, B_{12}, and protein I need. Then I check out my diet and decide, for example, that I should drink a glass of soy milk with dinner instead of water. I make an effort to add little things, like nuts sprinkled on salads, to enhance my diet."

soy versus cow's milk

When it comes to vitamin content, soy milk is not a substitute for cow's milk.

One cup of unfortified soy milk contains only about 10 milligrams of calcium; fortified brands like Eden and VitaSoy contain about 70 milligrams of calcium per cup. Soy milk does *not* contain any B_{12}. By comparison, fat-free cow's milk contains about 300 milligrams of calcium and about 1 microgram of B_{12} per cup.

Adolescents need about 1,300 milligrams of calcium and 2.4 micrograms of B_{12} every day. If you are substituting soymilk for cow milk, you need to get these nutrients from other foods.

"I learn a lot about nutrition from the cookbooks we have at our house. Some of them are especially helpful, because they give the nutritional values of individual foods. I must be doing something right, because I feel really healthy!"

"When I first started being vegetarian, I was very unhealthy. For example, instead of eating chicken, I had a candy bar. After six months of that, I didn't feel very healthy. If I feel energetic and my skin is clear, my hair is shiny, and my nails are strong, I know that I am healthy. That's the criteria I use to identify healthiness."

feel healthy, be healthy?

Feeling great does not reliably indicate the state of your health. Sure, feeling energetic and relaxed is a sign of good health. However, how you feel won't work as the only barometer of how healthy you are.

For example, you can feel just fine but have high blood pressure or be depleting bone mass because your calcium intake is low. In addition, low iron levels may not immediately make you feel tired.

Eating a balanced diet, getting physical exercise, and getting regular physical checkups are the best ways to keep your health in check.

"I took a nutrition class last year so I have a pretty good idea of what I should be eating, what food groups and how many calories. I don't pay much attention to calories, but I know that for protein I should be eating a lot of vegetables, tofu, nuts, beans, and some breads. I eat tons of carbohydrates, like pasta, rice, and couscous. Fat is everywhere, so it's really hard to avoid."

"Health is my second concern; the first one is animals. I'm not big into organic fruit, although I do support organic farming. I think organic is the best way to eat, but I can't afford to do it all the time. I would love to grocery shop at co-ops and health food stores, but regular grocery stores have a ton of food that I can eat for a lot cheaper. I'm so used to my vegan diet that it isn't a hassle anymore to figure out what I can and can't eat, or what I should eat. I've always taken multivitamin pills. Multivitamins have everything you need in them in case you don't have a healthy diet for a day or something. As for protein, most Americans get too much of it, which is actually bad for you. I get enough protein from soy, grains, and nuts. No problem."

where to find fat

Fat isn't everywhere. Most fruits and vegetables have no fat in them (avocados, coconut, and olives are a few exceptions). Grains and legumes are low in fat. These four food sources make up a large part of a healthy vegetarian diet.

For most Americans, more than 50 percent of dietary fat in their diet comes from eating meat, fish, poultry, eggs, and dairy products, and about 40 percent comes from butter, margarine, and oils.

While vegetarians generally eat diets that are lower in fat than nonvegetarians, eating too much fat on a vegetarian diet can still be an issue, especially if you are eating a pollo-, pesco-, lacto-, or ovo-vegetarian diet. So, even if you're a vegetarian, you should watch your fat intake so it remains about 30 percent or less of your total calories.

all protein bars are not created equal

Power and energy bars can be great snacks. Many are low in fat and are good sources of protein. They might contain a fair amount of simple sugars, however, which have little nutritional value and just add calories. All of these bars come in a variety of flavors, some tastier than others. Give them a try. They are healthful snacks that are easy to grab and go!

PowerBar:

230 calories, 2.5 grams fat, 3 grams fiber, 10 grams protein (milk protein), 20 grams sugar

LunaBar:

180 calories, 4 grams fat, 1 gram fiber, 10 grams protein (soy), 12 grams sugar

ClifBar:

250 calories, 6 grams fat, 5 grams fiber, 11 grams protein (soy), 20 grams sugar

Balance Bar:

200 calories, 6 grams fat, 1 gram fiber, 14 grams protein (soy), 17 grams sugar

"I take two calcium supplements daily. I also eat a protein bar every day that has 24 grams of protein. I have to take a vitamin B complex for the vitamins normally found in meat, and I eat a lot of spinach to make up for the iron I miss."

popeye is no nutritionist

Don't depend on spinach as your major source of iron.

Yes, spinach contains iron—1 cup of cooked spinach provides about 6 grams, and 1 cup of raw spinach contains about 1 gram. But spinach also contains oxalate, which binds with calcium and reduces the body's ability to absorb iron.

Soy products, whole grains, high-fiber foods, tea, and coffee are other iron sources that contain dietary factors that inhibit their absorption.

On the other hand, vitamin C (found in fruits and vegetables) helps the absorption of iron. If you love spinach, eat all you want. Just make sure you also eat a wide variety of other fruits and vegetables. Also, consider taking an iron supplement or eating iron-fortified cereal.

"I prefer to get my vitamins and minerals in the food I eat, rather than by taking supplements. In reality it doesn't always work out that way. So, I take calcium and B_{12} in pill forms. I also take flaxseed oil."

flaxseeds a health boost

Omega-3 fatty acids have been shown to reduce serum triglyceride levels (a form of fat that is transported in the body), reduce blood clots and to help reduce blood pressure. Omega-3 fatty acids are found in fish, fish oils and other seafoods. Vegetarian sources include soybeans, tofu, dark green leafy vegetables, walnuts and wheat germ. Recently, people have been turning to flaxseeds and flaxseed oil as excellent sources of omega-3. You can add ground flaxseeds to your food—just remember that it's important to grind them first in order to release the beneficial oils (try a coffee grinder). You'll find that they taste just like ground nuts. Or you can use flaxseed oil as a salad dressing, but note that it should not be heated. Heat will destroy all the "good stuff" in the oil.

"One winter, I got sick again and again with colds. My dad told me to start taking vitamins or eating more fruits and vegetables to boost my immune system. This health kick gradually turned into vegetarianism. When I have supper, I try to have different colors on my plate: a green, yellow and red vegetable. When I wake up and I say, 'Yes, I feel good today'; when I'm not tired, when I drink a lot of water, then I know I'm healthy."

color your dinner plate

Eating a rainbow of colorful fruits and vegetables is a great idea! Color is a good indicator that foods contain a lot of healthful nutrients.

The blue in blueberries, for example, comes from anthocyanidins; the orange in apricots, cantaloupe, and orange pepper means that carotenoids are present, and the red in tomatoes signals lycopene is around. The darker green the spinach and lettuce, the more vitamins there are.

These colors indicate protective factors against cancers and help to strengthen your immune system.

"I make sure to eat a good protein source at every meal—like eggs in the morning, a soy burger at lunch, and cheese pizza at dinner."

"I use my dad—the health freak—for information. When he became vegetarian, he researched everything and turned into a walking encyclopedia. If he perchance fails me, we have an entire library of vegetarian books. My mom went crazy, buying every book on the subject, because she was scared I wouldn't get enough protein."

Weight Loss: Automatic or Not?

Question: *Do you think vegetarianism helps people lose weight or maintain their weight?*

Replies:

"My sister lost about ten pounds when she became a vegetarian but gained it all back when she added fish to her diet. My weight stayed the same. I think whether you lose weight on a vegetarian diet depends on how you ate before the switch."

"I believe it helps people lose weight—absolutely. Meat has a lot of saturated fat. Plus, when you cut it out of your diet, you often replace it with healthier, lower-calorie foods."

"I'm a six-foot-tall, 175-pound male. I lost ten pounds when I initially became vegan. Now that I'm used to the diet, I maintain my new weight. Whether you are vegan or nonvegan, your weight depends on habits. If you exercise regularly, you will be able to maintain a healthy weight more easily. If you eat vegan potato chips and vegan cookies all day, you aren't going to lose any weight. An average vegan diet, though, is definitely healthier than a nonvegan diet. You can lose weight and also prevent a lot of diseases."

"For people who eat ground beef, salami, and highly processed/fatty foods, going vegetarian would help them cut out the bad fats and lose some weight. People accuse me of being small because of my vegetarian diet. I have always thought that is a ridiculous and offensive connection to draw, but now I see some truth in it. No, I don't have any "meat on my bones," and I'm proud of it!"

"I don't think that the switch to vegetarianism in and of itself helps someone lose or gain weight. Vegetarianism is a matter of *different* food, not necessarily less food. I think it can have an effect on weight, though, especially because you have to be more aware of what you're eating. For example, you might realize that you eat an entire bag of popcorn at the movies, and that's too much. It's like switching to any diet where you have to be a little more concerned about what you eat."

"It all depends on what you eat as a vegetarian. You could eat a lot of fatty snack foods. You could eat rich soy ice cream. You could eat guacamole every day. If the objective is weight loss, you've got to watch your fat and calories, not meat consumption."

soy ice cream facts

Soy milk ice cream is a popular non-dairy alternative to ice cream and frozen yogurt. Nutritionally, it is great because it is very low in saturated fat and has zero cholesterol. Unlike cow's milk, however, it is not a good source of calcium or protein. In fact, is not always a low-fat food.

Remember, it *is* dessert. Just like ice cream, soy ice cream is a "sometimes" food. If you're looking to cut down on calories and fat, and dairy is part of your diet, frozen yogurt is your best bet. Here are comparisons between three chocolate frozen desserts:

Chocolate Soy Dream:

140 calories, 7 grams fat, 0.5 grams saturated fat, 0 grams cholesterol, 11 grams sugar, 70 milligrams sodium, 1 gram protein, 0 grams calcium

Edy's Chocolate Ice Cream:

150 calories, 8 grams fat, 5 grams saturated fat, 115 milligrams cholesterol, 15 grams sugar, 35 milligrams sodium, 3 grams protein, 78 grams calcium

Edy's Chocolate Frozen Yogurt:

100 calories, 2.5 grams fat, 1.5 grams saturated fat, 10 milligrams cholesterol, 13 grams sugar, 30 milligrams sodium, 2 grams protein, 390 grams calcium

"Vegetarians find other ways to compensate for calories. For me, I eat a lot more pasta than I used to. I am constantly eating carbohydrates. It is more convenient and so much cheaper to eat more pasta and grains versus buying fresh fruit and vegetables. In this way, I don't know that becoming vegetarian would really help anyone lose weight. I would think it would make someone gain weight, not lose weight."

A Fringe Benefit

Question: *Did you decide to become vegetarian for any weight-related reason?*

Replies:

"I considered all the benefits of vegetarianism when I made the choice. And yes, weight loss was on the list, but it wasn't the only reason I switched."

healthy weight for teens

The healthiest weight for you depends on your height and your build. Your health-care provider is the best source for evaluating your weight. You can check out the Centers for Disease Control growth charts online (www.cdc.gov/growthcharts/) to get an idea of where your weight falls in relationship to other males and females your age.

"I'm a pretty slim person and I eat a lot. I became vegetarian because I hate the meat industry. I felt guilty eating animals."

"I wrote an essay when I became vegan and one of the sentences included, 'I think it's important that I don't grow up overweight because my father is a little overweight.' I would like to lead by example. Being a vegan at a healthy weight shows other people that veganism is a healthy choice for your body, as well as for the environment and animal rights."

"I know a lot of vegetarians who do it for weight control or weight loss alone, and I don't have much respect for that. To me, being vegetarian is an intensely political statement. It says, 'I want no part in the mistreatment of animals, and the industry has to change.'"

"I did lose weight when I first went vegan, but I gained a lot of it back this year. Since I'm already vegan and I think my diet is pretty good, I've decided to try to lose weight by exercising more. I'm running about three miles a day—the weight is starting to come off!"

a calorie is a calorie is a . . .

Eating a vegetable-based diet is not the secret to weight loss. Rather, eating a healthy diet combined with regular exercise is the key to maintaining a healthy weight. We gain weight when we consume more energy (calories) than we burn up. We burn up calories through growth, basic body processes like breathing and keeping our heart beating, and through being physically active. Excess calories from *any* source, animal, vegetable or Twinkie, can lead to weight gain.

Its recommended that adolescents get at least thirty minutes of moderate to vigorous physical activity—activities that get you moving such as brisk walking—at least 5 days each week and at least 20 minutes of vigorous activity—activities that really get your heart pumping and help you work up a sweat—3 days a week. Being physically active is a very important part of keeping your body healthy.

"I always felt like I was healthy, but in the first three months of being vegan, I lost thirty pounds. I never realized how much meat and buttery desserts I was eating. Now I know what it really feels like to be healthy! Weight loss wasn't the reason I became vegan, but an added bonus."

"I became vegan after I started valuing my health. I wanted to learn how to take better care of myself. I wanted to learn to love my body. Now I think of my body as a temple. I eat what will bring health, and what is not the result of someone's cruelty to animals. These ideas used to make me feel like an outcast, but now vegans are popping up all over the place. I saw a bumper sticker that said, 'Explore Veganism' and I thought, 'Yeah, I've explored veganism!'"

"I gained weight when I became a vegetarian, probably because of all the pasta and other empty calories I was eating. I also ate a lot of peanut butter sandwiches. Peanut butter has protein and 'good' unsaturated fat, but it's pretty high in calories."

"When I switched to being vegetarian, my lifestyle became more envi-ronmentally friendly and healthful in general. I lost weight, but it could have been the bike riding or the fact that I stopped drinking alcohol."

"I became vegetarian to lose weight, and I did—until I found more and more vegetarian foods that I loved. Now I'm back to my original weight."

The Opposite Problem

The following exchange took place in a chat group. It is about one teen's struggle to keep her weight on.

Subject: Need Some Help Keeping Weight On

"I'm having trouble keeping weight on. I need some guidance on what to eat, because my parents and whole family are really concerned. For example, this is what I ate yesterday:

Breakfast: two rice cakes, glass of skim milk

Lunch: ½ cup of fruit salad, small vegetable salad

Dinner: two bean tacos with refried beans, lettuce, and tomatoes on a spinach-flavored shell

Dessert: ½ cup of pineapple sorbet with two vanilla wafer cookies

P.S. I also exercise daily with sixty crunches and sixty jumping jacks. That little exercise shouldn't cause too much weight loss would it?"

she needs help alright!

We analyzed the diet of "Needs Some Help" using the nutritional factors you'll find in chapter 8, and here is what we found. On this typical day, she ate 549 calories, 27 grams of protein, 9 grams of fat (15 percent of her calories), 449 milligrams of calcium, 2.8 milligrams of iron, and 0.9 micrograms of vitamin B_{12}.

The bottom line? She is not meeting any of the dietary recommendations for calories, vitamins, and minerals. She isn't eating enough food to be healthy. The calorie intake is less than half of what she needs to maintain a healthy weight.

She may want to start by looking at the Vegetarian Food Guide Pyramid in chapter 2 to find some nutrient-dense foods and more calories to add to her diet. She definitely needs to make over her typical day's diet.

Finally, the crunches and jumping jacks are not burning enough calories to contribute to her weight loss.

Reply: Re: Need Some Help Keeping Weight On

You can go to fitday.com or to dieticians.ca (www.dietitians.ca/english/frames.html) and enter in everything that you ate on a typical day. It will tell you what nutritional value you got from your food. I wasn't getting enough calories for awhile, so I started adding one extra glass of juice each day. You might just need to make some minor adjust-ment like that. Or you might need to look past what you're eating for your weight loss. Are you under any sort of stress? You might not even know it consciously. Our bodies often feel emotional stress before our brains do. Anything like moving houses or schools, writing exams, fighting with siblings or parents, changing jobs, changing best friends, mean friends—even just worrying about the weight loss—can be enough for a person with a 'fast' metabolism to start losing weight. And, no, that amount of exercise shouldn't be making you lose much weight."

"Reply: Re: Need Some Help Keeping Weight On

Your dinner and dessert look balanced, but your breakfast and lunch need help. Meals should be balanced whenever possible. Your dinner contains protein (beans) and a carb (spinach wraps). Your breakfast needs to be bigger and more balanced. Try a whole-grain cereal with soy milk, rice milk, or cow's milk, and a piece of fruit. For a calorie boost top your cereal with nuts and raisins. For lunch eat a pb&j sand-wich on whole-grain bread or hummus along with your salad and fruit. Try and make sure that every meal contains a generous helping of a whole grain (bread, pasta, cereal, rice, etc.), a protein (beans, nuts, peanut butter, tofu, veggie burger, etc.), and then round it out with fruits and veggies. It would be great if we could live off of veggies and fruit, but if you don't want to look like a rail, it is a good idea to eat beans and grains every day."

"**Reply:** Re: Need Some Help Keeping Weight On

Well, some people have a really fast or slow metabolism, so what makes one person stay a 'normal' weight doesn't work for another. As far as lunch and breakfast go, here are some of my favorites that you might add to what you're already eating:

1. Whole-grain toast spread with nut butter/fruit preserves/hummus.
2. Power smoothies made with rice or soy or cow's milk blended with frozen strawberries and a banana. If you're daring, try adding some flaxseed oil, vitamin powder, protein powder, or wheat germ.
3. Healthy cereal with low-fat milk or fortified soy milk.
4. Scrambled tofu with sautéed mushrooms and green peppers.
5. And don't forget a nice tall glass of calcium-fortified OJ and/or some fresh fruit.

Lunch Idea

1. Salads are excellent but they should include some vegetarian protein; otherwise, they are too low in calories. Try tossing your favorite greens with chunks of tofu, almonds, sunflower seeds, chickpeas, some chopped veggies like baby carrots, celery, cucumbers, peppers, mushrooms, tomatoes, avocados, and a nice dressing.

Sandwich Ideas

Find a hearty, whole grain bread that you really like and fill your sandwich with:

1. Avocado, tomato, sprouts, and mayonnaise/vegenaise
2. Peanut butter and banana
3. Hummus and raw veggies with a nice spicy mustard
4. Peanut butter and raw radish (slice the radishes very fine)
5. Slices of tofu prepared with your favorite seasonings or sauce; don't forget the crisp lettuce and ripe tomato slices

Other things that are nice to take in lunches are Luna bars, rice cakes, pretzels, trail mix (try making your own; the store-bought kinds are usually oily, fatty, and sugary), granola, fresh raw veggies and a dip, big fresh apples, boxes of 100 percent juice."

Summing It Up

- Most of you became vegetarian gradually, not overnight.

- Although most of you did not become vegetarian or vegan in order to lose weight, many found that you did lose weight when you first switched to vegetarianism.

- Most of you said that weight control is one of the benefits of being a vegetarian.

- A few of you had trouble maintaining a normal weight and needed help from a professional as well as support from other vegetarians.

resources for a vegetarian life

BEING A VEGETARIAN IN A MEAT-BASED SOCIETY IS NOT ALWAYS EASY. WHERE CAN YOU GO FOR ADVICE AND SUPPORT? OTHER TEEN VEGETARIANS, OF COURSE! AFTER ALL, THAT IS WHAT THIS WHOLE BOOK IS ABOUT! BUT THE TEENS WHO CONTRIBUTED TO THIS BOOK HAVE MORE "OFFICIAL" SOURCES TO SUGGEST.

Many vegetarian teens are involved in organizations that support vegetarianism or are compatible with vegetarianism. These organizations, or membership in them, will not only help support you personally, they also help make our communities and society more vegetarian-friendly.

Strong Beliefs

Teens clearly believe there are health benefits to being vegetarian as well as benefits to the animals they are not eating. But we wanted to know how far they felt the benefits extended and what actions they took in their communities. The following questions address the potential for activism among vegetarian teens.

Question: *What kinds of benefits are there to your community or to society from becoming vegetarian?*

Replies:

"Vegans, in general, are more in tune with nature than their meat-eating counterparts. They are concerned with environmental issues and have a desire for peace in the world. Some vegans dream of a utopian society, where humans live in harmony with nature and are kind to each other as well as all living things. These beliefs can be so strong, and people can be so angry about the unnatural state of our society, that they are driven to social activism. Protesting can help instigate change, but it can also make others feel that vegans are disruptive and offensive. As a vegan myself, I was confused for a long time about why other people couldn't relate to my desire for peace and nature-friendly living. I learned, though, that shoving my beliefs down others' throats doesn't do anyone any good. The best way to show people what a peaceful, healthy choice veganism is, is by setting a peaceful, healthy example yourself."

"Vegans and vegetarians are usually sensitive to other issues besides just animal rights. They often care about human rights issues, like racial equality, feminism, and gay rights. Also, because vegetarianism is an alternate lifestyle choice itself, vegs tend to promote, and be very accepting of, diversity."

"As a vegetarian, I feel like a responsible member of my community. I know I'm a good person, in part because I don't contribute to the exploitation of animals. I think the entire community benefits from its vegetarian residents, especially when they organize clubs and groups that promote their morals."

"With every new vegetarian, the overall health of the community increases. If everyone cut back on their meat intake, or quit eating it altogether, there would probably be less heart disease, cancer, obesity, and diabetes in the community. Then less money would have to go to taking care of sick people, and more could go toward the arts, parks, schools, etc.!"

down with methane!

Methane, a colorless, odorless, flammable gas, is produced by the decomposition of organic matter (plants and animals) or from the mining and distribution of coal, oil, and gases. It is a concern for environmentalists and vegetarians for a couple of reasons.

First of all, it contributes to global warming. Heat enters the earth's atmosphere and is trapped by gases like methane. These gases absorb thermal radiation from the sun that would usually escape the earth's atmosphere. The more gas, the hotter it gets.

Secondly, 100 million tons of methane are released by cattle each year. Their stomachs break down and digest food, causing methane to be released in the form of burping and passing gas. And if the cattle's diet is poor, up to 40 percent more methane is released in the atmosphere.

Activism for Animals

How active are you in promoting your vegetarian lifestyle? Do you try and educate people about why and how you do it, or do you keep your mouth closed and hope nobody bugs you about it?

Question: *Are you involved in any organizations related to your vegetarianism?*

Replies:

"At the university I am exposed to a lot of student organizations, like SOAR (Students Organized for Animal Rights). They hand out pamphlets on street corners and sometimes organize student protests. I have learned a lot from them about the mistreatment of animals and about the false claims made by the meat industry. Big corporations use advertising to convince Americans that meat is a necessary part of a good diet. They show that meat makes us big and strong. In reality, meat is not necessary at all and can actually be a very unhealthy part of your diet. Yet the industry keeps trying to stuff if down our throats and telling us to buy more of it. Also, the grain that is fed to cows could be used to feed so many more humans. When there are people in the world dying of starvation, I think we should make sure to feed *them* before we feed the cattle we plan to fatten up and then kill. Plus, cattle contribute to methane pollution."

"SOAR is the oldest animal rights group in the city. We've been around for thirteen years. SOAR used to be really radical. In its heyday, as many as fifty people came to the meetings. Now we're a bit smaller, but we're getting the word out to high school students and colleges nearby. SOAR has always been a big proponent of direct action. We have speakers come in to organize protests and provide information for people who want to get involved. We make ourselves seen in public."

"I've been influenced by Vegan Outreach, which focuses on the animal rights aspect. If you don't focus on animal rights, many people will continue to wear fur and covet leather goods. I do my best to educate people by focusing on the issue that is closest to their heart. For example, if they care about wildlife, I talk about how meat production harms the environment. I talk about the importance of sustainable agriculture, and how vegetarianism is a big step towards ending hunger. If their principle concern is personal health, I educate them on the harmful effects of meat's cholesterol and saturated fat. If I'm talking to a woman with a lot of babies, or a school teacher, I explain the diseases that are distributed by meat products in school cafeterias. Kids have died from salmonella, and irradiated meat has caused problems, too."

the way to grow

Sustainable agriculture is a system of agricultural production and distribution that seeks to minimize negative impacts on health, safety, wildlife, water quality, and the environment. Examples of how this is achieved include limiting the use of nonrenewable resources, integrating natural biological cycles into production, and promoting opportunities in family farming and farm communities.

To learn more about the importance of sustainable agriculture and how to get involved, check out SARE (Sustainable Agriculture Research and Education) at www.sare.org.

"SOAR is less about veganism and more about animal rights. As a member of that group, I'm involved in designing effective strategies for communicating with people in a protest-type situation. We provide information on the vegan diet, but our main concern is the larger animal rights issue. There is another animal rights group called MARCH (Movement for Animal Rights by Concerned Humans). MARCH focuses more on outreach and showing people that vegetarian and vegan lifestyles and diets are viable. With that group there are more potlucks, which expose people to vegan food and help them meet others who are making the switch."

"I'm helping to start an animal rights caucus in the Green Party. When I was in high school, I was the leader of the animal rights committee. I organized projects to educate myself and the other kids in my school, as well as our community. For example, we took a trip to a dairy farm that had about 3,000 cows. I think it's a lot more powerful to see things firsthand than to read about them in books."

"I'm part of Amnesty International, which is an organization that works parallel to the animal rights groups. We distribute an animal rights newsletter, and we organize protests that occasionally include animal rights issues. I've never been involved in a violent protest; I've never thrown things at people eating at McDonald's, for example."

"Vegetarianism is so important to me, and so much a part of my identity, that I forget other people eat meat. I don't preach about my lifestyle, or try to convert people; vegetarianism is just a part of my life. I attended a vegetarian conference in Berkeley and was shocked by how actively other kids my age are promoting the vegetarian diet. They hand out millions of pamphlets and do whatever they can to get the word out about the evilness of meat. I think it's relatively difficult to convince another person to go vegetarian. I think it's a choice you have to come to on your own. When you decide to learn more about it, there are plenty of places to search out information.

A Spiritual Connection

Many adult vegetarians find their support through their personal beliefs, faith, or spirituality. Some find it through an organized religion. For example, some religions, such as Hinduism and Buddhism, promote a vegetarian diet for spiritual purposes. We wondered if younger vegetarians feel the same connection, so we asked the following:

Question: *Does your vegetarianism relate to your faith or spiritual beliefs?*

Replies:

"I have never thought about being a vegetarian in the context of my faith, but I have a story to share about it. I work with a really cool guy who is the typical meat-eating male. He lives on meat and potatoes. But he has always been really curious about why I'm a vegetarian. He asks me questions about my diet all the time. Then, yesterday he told me he wanted to go vegetarian for one week, just to see what it's like. I was so excited! He's eliminated meat in his diet and he's eating like I eat every day. When people ask him how he does it, he attributes it to his faith. For him, he's eliminated meat as a kind of fasting. When he thinks about meat, wants meat, or is finding it rough to stay meatless, he will pray and tell me, 'You gotta get me through this.' I really respect him for that."

"I am not formally a Taoist, but I use some of their principles in my daily life. As a vegetarian, I feel I live more in harmony with nature. I feel more balanced. I respect animals as living, feeling beings, and therefore do not contribute to their killing."

"I think it's wrong to eat another living creature. From a biological standpoint as well as a historical standpoint, though, people have been doing it for thousands of years. If I had to kill my own animals to eat, and had to use the rest of their bodies to make tools and clothing, that would be one thing. But now that animal mistreatment is widespread and meat has to be mass-produced, I have moral issues with meat eating. If I had to kill a chicken to survive, for example, I would recognize that I am taking a life and therefore do it with a great deal of respect. I can't eat frozen chicken nuggets out of a box, though, knowing what the chicken went through."

religious views of vegetarianism

If anyone tries to tell you that certain religions advocate eating meat, quote the following:

Buddha: "All creatures love life. All creatures fear death. Therefore do not kill or cause another to kill."

The Old Testament (Genesis 1:27–31): "He created them male and female, blessed them, and said, 'Have many children, so that your descendants will live all over the earth and bring it under their control. I am putting you in charge of the fish, the birds, and all the wild animals. I have provided all kinds of grain and all kinds of fruit for you to eat; but for all the wild animals and for all the birds I have provided grass and leafy plants for food'—and it was done. God looked at everything he had made, and he was very pleased."

Saint Francis of Assisi: "Not to hurt our humble brethren (the animals) is our first duty to them, but to stop there is not enough. We have a higher mission—to be of service to them whenever they require it. If you have men who will exclude any of God's creatures from the shelter of compassion and pity, you will have men who will deal likewise with their fellow men."

Doing Your Homework

There is no shortage of information out there on vegetarianism. Which are the most helpful books? Does the web have the most up-to-date information?

Question: *Where do you get information to inform your vegetarianism?*

Replies:

GO ONLINE

"I use the Internet to find answers to my questions. You can type keywords into Google, and so many sites will pop up that you won't know where to start. I find veganstore.com especially helpful when I need new hygiene products. The problem with the Internet is that not all the information is true. I suggest checking to see if the site is provided by an accredited source, or if it's just some guy in his basement making things up."

READ, READ, READ

"I read *Animal Liberation* by Peter Singer and refer back to that pretty often. I also get a newsletter from Vegan Outreach. A lot of my resources, though, are people I know. Some of my vegan friends and I have formed a club; if one of us has a question or concern, usually at least one other person has an answer."

"I read magazines like *Animal Agenda*, those from PETA, *Animal Times*, and other underground animal liberation periodicals. I think it's important to see the issues from many different angles, so I also read farm journals and information put out by the National Dairy Council and the meat industry."

FIND OUT WHAT'S COOKIN'

"When I became a vegan, my parents bought me two cookbooks. They helped me find foods I could eat and also gave me nutrition information. Once I figured out how to eat a healthy vegan diet, I expanded my horizons to include animal rights activism. I've found that most organizations provide pamphlets and information packets that are really helpful. Some even have recipes and recommendations for other helpful sources. The success of their organization depends on the actions and number of their members, so they want to help vegans stick to their lifestyle."

"The book *Vegetarian Cooking for Dummies*, by Suzanne Havala, is my favorite resource. It's really easy to navigate and has good nutrition information."

"I have a few vegetarian cookbooks filled with bland recipes. I prefer cookbooks that focus on a particular ethnic cuisine, like Thai or Indian. Even though they include meat, I know enough about alternatives to choose an appropriate meat substitute. Too many people think vegetarian food has to be boring. That's not true at all! I also find a lot of good information for vegans in *Shape* magazine. They have articles on nutrition, fitness, and general well-being."

authors' best picks

There are other resources besides the ones listed in this chapter that we use ourselves. These are some of the ones we like the best.

Grocery store frozen vegetarian foods:

- Amy's brand (www.amys.com; vegan or lacto-)
- DEEP (www.deepfoods.com; vegan or lacto- Indian food)
- Boca burgers (www.bocaburger.com; lacto-ovo)
- MorningStar Farms (www.kelloggs.com/brand/msfarms/home.html; lacto-ovo)

Online vegetarian foods:

- www.vegecyber.com (vegetarian meat substitutes, primarily vegan)
- www.vrg.org (the Vegetarian Resource Group; provides information on alternative foods)
- www.thevegetariansite.com/index.htm (vegetarian products, including food and clothing)

"I have three vegetarian cookbooks that I use a lot: *Forever Summer*, by Nigella Lawson; *Vegetarian Treasure Chest*, by Winifred Graham; and the *Moosewood Cookbook*, by Mollie Katzen."

Best on the Web

Question: *What are the best websites for vegetarians between the ages of twelve and twenty?*

Postings:

"I believe PETA (www.peta.com) to be the best website choice. They have a plethora of information on nutrient requirements, facts about the ill effects of animal products on the body, details of the horrors of the meat and dairy industry, revealing information about the intelligence of animals, a recipe center, a support system, boards, and an animal activism group that has rewards—an all-around fantastic site."

"veganoutreach.com is the best! I love it; their literature helped me go veg. PETA has excellent sites; peta2.com is great for connecting activists and motivating everyone. GoVeg.com is a good one, too."

"www.vegetarianteen.com is cool. They have information for lacto-ovo, vegan, and raw. You can talk to other people your age about problems with your diet, exchange recipes, and even meet people. I mostly use the PETA websites, though, because they tend to have the most information, and there are so many of them."

"I love vegweb.com, because it has loads of recipes. I also like the message board at govegan.net."

Good Reading

Question: *What are your favorite cookbooks, books, and magazines related to vegetarianism?*

Postings:

"I love *Vegan Vittles*, by Joanne Stepaniak and Suzanne Havala. It contains not only recipes but stories about rescued animals as well. It's a touching read."

"*How It All Vegan*, by Sarah Kramer and Tanya Barnard, *The Meat and Potato Vegetarian Cookbook*, and *The Uncheese Cookbook*, by Joanne Sepaniak. All of those are great."

"I love *The Jewish Vegetarian Year Cookbook*, by Roberta Kalechofsky and Rosa Rasiel! It's basically vegan, and they have a ton of recipes that are good for veganizing traditional Jewish holidays."

"My favorite cookbooks have to be *How It All Vegan* and *The Garden of Vegan*, both by Sarah Kramer and Tanya Barnard. They're so easy to follow and have some great recipes, and they also help you convert other recipes by giving suggestions for egg substitutes. Apart from that, I like *Vegan Feasts*, by Rose Elliot. It's not as good as some, but it's clear and has some good ideas. Also *The Milk Free Kitchen*, by Beth Kidder and Harold M. Friedman, is good as well. I also use normal cookbooks and change the recipes to make them vegan."

The Final Word

Question: *If you were going to give advice to another teen on becoming vegetarian, what would you say?*

Replies:

"Educate yourself. Look at all the sources, look at everything critically. Learn about what's out there. Familiarize yourself with the foods you can eat. Now that I look back, it was pretty simple to become vegetarian. There are a lot of vegetarians in our society already, so you can find a lot of foods in stores and in restaurants. It's a little more difficult to be vegan; you have to familiarize yourself with the options that are out there. There are more than you think—you just have to start looking! Actually, what I've learned by being vegan is that you educate yourself so much that you discover different kinds of foods that you never knew were out there. Whenever you have doubts, or feel like it's too hard to be vegan, think about all the good you're doing for animals."

"We always talk about battles in the world and choosing your battles, but veganism isn't a lifetime battle. You can conquer veganism by learning to do it healthfully. It's animal liberation that is a lifetime battle. Sometimes people say, 'Veganism is a picky, upper-class thing to do.' And sure, it may seem like it at first glance. People in the upper class can afford to buy organic and shop at health food stores. But there are plenty of cheap ways to live the vegan lifestyle and plenty of people who do it. By eating a vegan diet, you have a direct effect on the economy. You've actually lowered your eating on the food chain. You consume fewer resources than you would if you ate meat. My advice to other vegans is: Stay with it! You *are* making a difference."

"Have patience with yourself. If you're having trouble completely avoiding meat, remind yourself that every piece of meat you *don't* eat is helping. Don't beat yourself up over the little bit of meat that you do eat. Remember: The longer you go without something, the less you want it. It may someday be the same way with dairy products. You might decide to avoid them, too. I'm a big proponent of goal setting. Tell yourself, 'I'm going to go for a day as a vegan.' You'll see that it isn't very difficult to do. Then try it for three days, and then try it for a week. Pretty soon, you'll say, 'This cheese is nasty and I can't eat it.' You'll have stopped liking foods you used to think you couldn't live without!"

"I think it's best to go cold turkey. Cut the meat totally out of your diet and the cravings will disappear after just a few days. You'll have to have strong will power. Tell the people around you that you're doing it, and ask them to support you. Also, find a bunch of interesting recipes. It'll be hard to stick to a vegan diet that consists of salad for every meal."

"Whoever you are, you will get teased by some person for some thing. And you have to accept that that's going to happen. I've accepted that I get teased about my political views and my vegetarianism. There are a lot of people that agree with me—most of my friends. So I don't get teased by them. I get teased by other people in class when I express my views. You can try to defend yourself, but it's not going to be worth it in the long run. Just pay close attention to the nature of the teasing; if it becomes harassment, deal with it appropriately."

"Make vegetarianism fun by cooking new recipes for your friends and family. If your parents subscribe to *Cooking Light* magazine, you can access their online recipe database. There are thousands of recipes to choose from!"

Summing It Up

- You have and are willing to share ideas with other teens who might want to switch to a vegetarian diet.

- It is best to do a lot of research in order to get the facts.

- There are social and community reasons for being a vegetarian which are important to many of you.

- Many of you have joined community groups to support animal rights and the protection of the environment.

- You get your information primarily from the Internet, from cookbooks, and from magazines. Some of you are members of national and local organizations that support your vegetarianism.

getting your
food right

AS A TEEN, YOU ARE FACED WITH SOME MAJOR NUTRI-TIONAL ISSUES WHEN YOU TURN TO A VEGETABLE-BASED DIET. THAT'S BECAUSE THE WONDERFUL HEALTH BENEFITS OF A VEGETARIAN DIET CAN ONLY BE GARNERED BY MAKING SURE YOUR DIET IS BRIMMING WITH ESSENTIAL NUTRIENTS. CONVERSELY, FOLLOWING AN UNSOUND DIET CAN HAVE SOME UNPLEASANT CONSEQUENCES.

Some of these nutritional issues have come up in this book several times—things like finding adequate amounts of protein, iron, and vitamin B_{12}, getting ample calcium and vitamin D in the absence of dairy, and taking in enough calories to sustain a healthy weight. Nutrition, however, is so important that we feel it is necessary to focus an entire chapter on it.

We deviate here from the teen-to-teen advice approach of this book in order to give you a professional, soup-to-nuts, what-you-need-to-know lesson in vegetarian nutrition. Following the "nutrition lesson," we'll take a look at several typical vegetarian menus based on true diets submitted to us by some of the teens who participated in this book. We'll tweak these menus—or overhaul them, if necessary—to show you just how easy it is to make your diet as healthy—and tasty—as possible.

The Vegetarian Nutrition Gospel

If you are just starting on a vegetarian diet, though, you are probably being bombarded with information and misinformation from well-meaning parents and friends. It's enough to give you a Big Mac attack! We don't want that to happen. So we're here to give it to you straight—everything you need to know about making your vegetarian experience a nutritionally sound one.

CALORIES: THE STARTING POINT

Calories are not just an issue for vegetarian teens. They are an issue for all teens and all adults. Some vegetarian teens, however, do struggle with their weight—both keeping it up and keeping it from getting out of control. Getting your weight right is a matter of knowing how many calories you need.

Calories, simply, are the ways that we count the amount of fuel that is in the food we eat. Scientists refer to calories as energy or kilocalories (kcal), so if you see these words in your own reference reading, consider the three words synonymous. Calories, or energy, have three main functions. We need to consume calories so that we have enough energy to:

- maintain basic physiological processes such as breathing and circulating blood

- digest our food

- be physically active

Teens need additional energy or calories to grow. And everyone needs additional calories to stay warm in cold temperatures or deal with a trauma such as surgery or an injury. To make sure everyone is on the same page, the federal government has designed what it calls the Recommended Dietary Allowance (RDA)—target numbers for a healthy existence. For calories, this number is 2,500 for males ages eleven to fourteen and 3,000 for males ages fifteen to eighteen. Females need approximately 2,200 calories through adulthood. But these are just rough estimates. Let's take a closer look.

The energy that we need just keep our body working—heart beating, lungs expanding and contracting, and blood circulating, for example—is called our Resting Energy Expenditure (REE). About 60 to 75 percent of the calories we eat go to maintaining our REE. Another 10 percent goes toward digesting our food, and 15 to 30 percent is used to move around and be physically active. One's REE is determined by age, gender, and body composition. In general, younger people need more energy than older people; males need more energy than females; and people who are leaner or have more muscle need more energy than people who are not so lean. The following table shows you how to estimate your REE.

calculate your REE!—the calories you need to stay alive

1. Calculate your body weight in kilograms
   - Divide your weight in pounds by 2.2 (kilograms/pound). This gives you your weight in kilograms.
2. Determine your Resting Energy Expenditure (REE)
   - For males ages 10–18: (17.5 x weight in kilograms) + 651 = REE
   - For females ages 10–18; (12.2 x weight in kilograms) + 746 = REE

So, for males, multiply your weight in kilograms by 17.5 and then add 651. For females, multiply your weight in kilograms by 12.2 and then add 746. These calculations will give you your REE!

Not many of us, however, just sit in a chair and breathe! We all move around to some extent, and any additional movement requires more energy. Use your REE and your activity factor to estimate how many calories you need to eat daily. (The activity factor includes the calories that you need to digest your food.)

your total calorie needs: REE and physical activity

Your total calorie needs are equal to your REE multiplied by the activity factors listed below.

Activity Factor		Activity Level	Description
male	female		
1.3	1.3	Sedentary	• Mostly sitting (watching television, playing video games, talking on the phone.
1.6	1.5	Light	• Occasional Activity (walking at the mall, walking between classes)
1.7	1.6	Moderate	• Daily regular activity (riding bikes, jogging or walking fast, playing an active sport)
2.1	1.9	Heavy	• Daily vigorous activity requiring several hours of continuous activity (playing competitive sports)

EXAMPLE: CATE

Cate weighs 120 pounds and does not get any regular activity. She walks around school, and it is only a short walk to her bus stop. She rarely breaks into a sweat or moves about for any length of time. How many calories does she need to maintain her weight?

1. First we calculate her weight in kilograms: 120 pounds divided by 2.2 kilograms per pound = 54.5 kilograms (kg).

2. Next we calculate her REE which is (12.2 x 54.5 kg)+ 746 = 1,411 kcal. So, if she just sits in a room and breathes, she will need about 1,400 calories to stay alive.

3. Finally, we account for her level of physical activity, which is light: 1,411 calories x 1.5 = 2,117 calories. Cate needs to eat an estimated 2,117 calories every day to maintain her weight at her current level of activity. If she starts being more physically active, her calorie needs will increase.

Calories (energy) are found in the protein, fat, and carbohydrates that we consume. Water, vitamins, and minerals contain no calories.

If we eat more calories than we need to grow or just keep alive and move around (REE), we will store the excess calories as body fat. The excess calories that are stored as fat can come from protein, fat, or carbohydrate. Your body can't recognize the source! If you do not eat enough calories to maintain your body's needs, your body will begin burning calories that are stored as fat. Once your fat stores are depleted, your body will break down body protein, such as muscles, for fuel.

One pound of body fat is formed for every excess 3,500 calories consumed. That means that if you eat an extra 500 calories a day for a week (500 calories x 7 days), your body would store 1 pound of fat. On the other side, if you were in a calorie deficit of 500 calories a day for a week, you would lose 1 pound of body fat.

Vegetarian teens need to make sure they are eating enough calories for normal growth and development and to fuel their activity needs, but not so many that they store excess body fat.

THE PROTEIN PROBLEM AND SOLUTION

Parents have a lot of reasons to question their teens' conversion to vegetarianism. We've heard plenty about this already in this book! One concern is that their teens won't get enough protein if they don't eat meat.

The American culture associates meat with protein and no wonder! The average American gets about 65 percent of dietary protein from animal products. Other cultures, however, have done just fine relying on plants as their major protein source. In Africa and Asia, plant sources provide about 80 percent of the protein in the diet.

Another concern is getting what is known as "complete protein." Complete proteins contain all the essential amino acids that a body needs to nurture muscle, bone, enzymes, hormones and other life-sustaining functions.

Proteins serve many functions. They are essential elements in our body's structure and movement. Bone, skin, hair, and muscle all contain proteins. They are also part of the antibodies our body produces to help ward off infections and help make up enzymes and hormones. Proteins help maintain fluid balance and keep cells in working order. If the diet does not provide enough energy for vital functions, stored protein in the body can be broken down to provide that energy.

The RDA for protein is based on body size. For adolescents, it is recommended that for every kilogram of weight, between 0.8 to 1.0 grams of protein are needed daily. Using pounds instead of kilograms, that translates into 0.4 grams of protein for every pound you weigh. Protein should make up about 10 percent of the energy in the total diet. Eating more protein than that will probably mean that some of the protein consumed will be used as an extra source of energy or calories. Most Americans get plenty of protein in their diet; excessive protein becomes an expensive source of energy or ends up as stored body fat!

WHERE'S THE PROTEIN?

If you are a lacto-ovo, lacto, ovo, pesco- or pollo- vegetarian, getting enough protein will not be an issue for you as long as you eat enough calories. Vegetarians who eat some animal products will automatically get enough protein, and the protein that they eat will be complete. The only plant food that contains complete protein is soy. If you are a vegetarian who regularly includes soy products in your diet (soy milk, soy flour, tofu, etc.), you will be getting complete protein and have few protein worries!

If you are a vegan and do not regularly consume soy products, then you'll need to be a bit more careful about menu planning. Most plant proteins are incomplete proteins, meaning that they do not include all the essential amino acids or don't include them in the correct proportions to make them as useful for the body's protein needs. You'll need to mix and match different protein sources within a day to make sure that your body gets the protein that it needs. Below is a list of some foods that will provide complementary proteins.

Complementary proteins are formed when two or more foods made up of incomplete proteins are combined and together supply all the essential amino acids. We used to believe that these complementary protein foods had to be eaten at the same meal, but more current research shows that as long as the complementary protein foods are eaten in the same day, protein needs in the body will not suffer.

THE FAT FACTS

Fat is considered a dietary nasty, but we need some fat it our diet. The typical diet Americans eat provides too much fat, which is contributing to the high rate of heart disease, some cancers, and obesity we are experiencing in this country. The villain responsible for this is saturated fat, and it is found in animal products. If you are a vegan, getting too much fat in your diet is probably not a concern. If you are a vegetarian who consumes some animal products, you need to pay attention.

Dietary fat is essential for providing body fuel. Gram for gram, dietary fat provides twice as many calories (9 calories per gram) than carbohydrates and protein (both provide 4 calories per gram). Dietary fat is a primary source of vitamins A, D, E, and K, which are called fat-soluble vitamins. Fat also provides satiety, meaning that it helps us to feel full and satisfied after a meal. A diet that has no fat in it can be very hard to swallow!

Fat requirements are based on the calories that we eat. No more than 30 percent of our calories should come from fat. For example, if you eat 2,000 calories in a day, no more than 600 calories (2000 kcal multiplied by 0.30 = 600) should come from fat. Since there are 9 calories per gram of fat, that means that your diet should include no more than about 66 grams of fat each day.

There are different kinds of fat in the foods that we eat. Saturated fats, which we already mentioned, are primarily found in animal products. Certain unsaturated fats found in nonmeat products have been found to be protective against certain diseases. For example, monounsaturated fats (found in olives, peanuts, and walnuts) and polyunsaturated fats (found in most vegetable oils) are believed to help prevent heart disease. Flaxseed contains omega-3 fatty acids that help lower cholesterol and may help reduce the risk of some cancers. The saturated fats in animal products, on the other hand, are associated with increased risk for heart disease.

Some healthier vegetable fats undergo a process called hydrogenation and are used in margarines and processed snack products. This process transforms these healthier fats into unhealthy "transfatty acids" that can increase the risk of certain diseases.

If you are a vegan, saturated fats are not an issue in your diet. If you are not vegan, then limiting the amount of higher-fat animal products (such as whole milk, cheese, and eggs) will help you keep your saturated fat intake down. Reducing the amount of processed foods in your diet also will keep your intake of transfatty acids down.

There are a few foods that do not contain any fats, including most fruits and vegetables. Avocados and olives are two of the few exceptions, though they contain the healthy monounsaturated kind of fat. Animal products contain fat, unless it has been removed. For example, skim milk has had all of its butterfat removed. Seeds, nuts, and grains contain some fat, but most do not contain harmful saturated fat.

THE CALCIUM CHALLENGE

Calcium is one nutrient that most teens, vegetarian and nonvegetarian alike, have trouble getting in adequate amounts. Bone-building calcium is especially important during periods of growth, so all teens need to know a thing or two about his meat.

Calcium is the major component of bones and teeth. It is also essential for muscle contraction, nerve impulse transmission, blood clotting, and regulation of cell metabolism. Stable blood calcium levels are so important that calcium will be pulled from bones and muscle if blood calcium levels get too low.

Bone mineralization is greatest during growth periods and about five to ten years after growth has stopped. Therefore, adolescence is a crucial time to lay down bone and a critical time to meet calcium requirements. Teens who have chronic and severely inadequate calcium intakes may not grow to their optimal height. Those who have not consumed adequate calcium during adolescence are at greater risk for developing osteoporosis (a disease that causes bones to become weak and brittle) during adulthood.

Both males and females teens need 1,300 milligrams of calcium daily.

WHERE'S THE CALCIUM?

In the United States and Canada, milk and dairy products are the most common sources of calcium. One 8-ounce glass of cow's milk provides about 300 milligrams of calcium. Other nondairy sources of calcium include calcium-processed tofu, kale, greens, Chinese cabbage, broccoli, and calcium-fortified orange juice.

Calcium sources vary in their bioavailability (how easily the body can absorb and use a nutrient). Depending on the source, we absorb between 25 to 75 percent of the calcium we eat. While we can absorb about one-third of the calcium in cow's milk, we can only absorb about 5 percent of the calcium in spinach. For example, when we drink 1 cup of milk, we are able to absorb about 150 milligrams, or half of what is present in the milk. When we eat ½ cup of spinach, we are eating about 120 milligrams of calcium, but our body absorbs only about 6 milligrams.

The following conditions influence calcium availability:

- Excessive protein intake increases calcium losses.

- Large quantities of wheat bran, whole grains, nuts and seeds inhibit calcium absorption.

- Vitamin D enhances calcium absorption.

So what is a teen to do? Teen vegetarians who eat dairy products need to consume at least three servings of dairy products daily (the low-fat versions are your best bet) and eat a variety of calcium-rich vegetables. Vegan teens need to be sure to eat a variety of foods. Eating an excess of healthful foods like whole grains and nuts is not a good idea because the excess grains may inhibit calcium absorption. Drinking calcium-fortified soy milk and eating calcium-processed tofu and a variety of calcium-rich vegetables will help ensure that calcium requirements are being met.

Calcium supplements are another option. Unlike most mineral and vitamin supplements, it is best to take calcium supplements between meals, not with meals. Do not take more than 2,500 milligrams of calcium daily, because doing so may interfere with the absorption of other minerals, including zinc.

animal-free calcium sources

The following animal-free calcium sources provide bioavailable calcium equivalent to one glass of cow's milk.

Broccoli	2.5 cups
Kale	1.75 cups
Mustard greens	1.33 cups
Turnip greens	1 cup
Chinese cabbage	1 cup
Tofu processed with calcium	.5 cups
Calcium-fortified orange juice	5 ounces

(Adapted from Insel, Turner and Ross, 2003)

IRON WILL BE FOUND

Iron deficiency is the most common nutrient deficiency in the world, probably due to two things: inadequate overall intake of foods that contain iron and the inability to absorb the iron in the foods that are eaten. Vegetarians are at risk for iron deficiency because they can fall into both categories.

Iron is important because it is the essential transporter of oxygen in the blood. It is also an essential component in enzymes and plays a role in energy metabolism, brain development, and the immune system.

Iron requirements are greatest for females who menstruate because monthly blood loss results in iron loss. The iron recommendation for adolescent girls ranges from 8 to 15 milligrams and increases to18 milligrams once a female reaches age nineteen. For adolescent males, the recommended levels range from 8 to 11 milligrams.

WHERE'S THE IRON?

Iron is a lot like calcium when it comes to the body's ability to absorb it. Red meat has always been considered the prime source of iron because it is rich in heme iron, the form of the mineral that is most readily available—that is, the easiest to absorb. In fact, animal products are the only source of heme iron. Vegetables contain solely nonheme iron, which is less readily available. This does not mean, however, that vegetarians will become iron deficient. It means that they have to eat more of the delicious iron-containing vegetables, fruits, and legumes. These include lentils, kidney beans, garbanzo beans, pinto beans, seitan, sesame seeds, raisins, and some tofu. Not all tofu is the same; you will need to check the nutrition label for information on the product's iron content.

Iron absorption depends on a number of things including the body's iron state (absorption increases when iron stores are low), how the gastrointestinal tract is functioning (some blood is lost via the gastrointestinal tract), and the amount and type of iron in the diet.

Other factors that influence the availability of iron include the following:

• Vitamin C increases iron absorption.

• Whole grains can decrease iron absorption.

• Tea, coffee, soybeans, high-fiber foods, and oxalates can inhibit iron absorption. (Oxalates are organic acids that are found in some leafy green vegetables, such as spinach, which bind to calcium to form calcium oxalate, an insoluble compound the body cannot absorb.)

Vegetarians can ensure that they get adequate iron in their diet by including a good source of vitamin C (found in most fruits and vegetables) with every meal and by eating foods fortified with iron. When in doubt, take a multiple vitamin/mineral supplement that includes iron. Overdoses of iron can be very dangerous, especially to small children. Keep your supplements away from younger siblings and stick to lower-dose multivitamin/mineral supplements.

GUNNING FOR VITAMIN B_{12}

Vitamin B_{12} is another vegetarian issue because it can only be found in animal foods. Though we need very little—only 2.4 micrograms a day—it is important because it helps make red blood cells and provides a protective coating around nerve fibers. A prolonged deficiency of vitamin B_{12} can cause pernicious anemia and even nerve damage. Both are very serious conditions, so you must take your B_{12} seriously.

All naturally occurring B_{12} comes from bacteria. Animals contain B_{12} because they get it from bacteria on their food. It is also produced in their intestinal tracts. While in the past vitamin B_{12} may have been available from bacteria from our food, it is much less likely to occur given current farming practices and food production systems. You may have read that you can get B_{12} from tempeh, miso, or sea vegetables, but most experts agree that those sources are not reliable.

If you eat any animal products (including any dairy or eggs), you don't need to worry about getting B_{12} in your diet. If you are a vegan, you need to plan carefully how to get B_{12}. The most reliable sources are fortified breakfast cereals, fortified soy products, other foods fortified with B_{12}, a multivitamin supplement, and nutritional yeast.

Other dietary issues you need to pay attention to are vitamin D, zinc, fiber, and sugar.

Vitamin D is a fat-soluble vitamin that is needed for calcium absorption. Vitamin D is not a natural component of any food; we get it from exposure to the sun. Anyone who does not eat vitamin D–fortified foods and does not get exposure to sun may experience a vitamin D deficiency.

If you don't eat vitamin D–fortified foods (most dairy products are fortified with vitamin D), make sure that you are spending some time outdoors every day—as little as 10 to 30 minutes will do. This does not mean you have to sunbathe to get your vitamin D. Just being outdoors will work. Skip the sunscreen for this "vitamin D bath." Even sunscreen with an SPF of 8 will block vitamin D synthesis.

Zinc is a component of enzymes and is essential to cell division. It also plays a part in taste sensation. Zinc is found in seeds, nuts, legumes, and sprouts. While the zinc intake of the general population is lower than recommended, intakes of some vegans are extremely low. It appears that when a zinc deficiency occurs, it is often due to nutrients competing with zinc for absorption. For example, calcium supplements inhibit zinc absorption, and foods that are very high in fiber may inhibit zinc absorption as well.

the OJ challenge

A health-conscious vegetarian should forego soft drinks and reach for fruit juice instead. A 12-ounce Coca Cola, for example, for gives you a big dose of sugar (15 teaspoons of it to be exact!), while calcium-fortified orange juice provides carbohydrates and calories but lots of other benefits as well. Added sugars should provide no more than 10 percent of your daily calories.

	12 Oz. COCA COLA	12 Oz. ORANGE JUICE
Total Calories	240	105
Carbohydrates (grams)	60	39
Added Sugar (grams)	60	0
Vitamin C (milligrams)	0	162
Calcium (milligrams)	0	525

Vegans can make sure that they are getting enough zinc by ensuring that their calorie intake is adequate; by increasing their intake of sprouts and fermented soy foods such as tempeh and miso; by increasing their intake of nuts and seeds; or by eating zinc-fortified foods.

Fiber is another nutrient that is important to teens. Fiber is a carbohydrate that gives plant cells their structure. Fiber is different from other carbohydrates because it cannot be broken down during digestion. Foods particularly rich in fiber include whole-grain foods like brown rice; legumes such as kidney beans, peas and lentils; fruits; and vegetables. Fiber is an important part of everyone's diet because it promotes regular bowel function, and also helps adjust and regulate blood cholesterol and blood sugar.

For a vegetarian teen eating a healthy diet full of fruits, veggies, whole grains, and protein-rich plant sources, getting enough fiber should be no problem. The recommended intake of fiber for teens, males and females, is 15 grams daily.

Sugar is another form of carbohydrate in the diet and one that most teens and adults get way too much of! While all carbohydrates provide 4 calories per gram, the sweetness found in white and brown sugar, honey, and syrups provides those calories with little or no nutritional benefit.

A MESSAGE ABOUT SUPPLEMENTS

Taking a multivitamin/mineral supplement daily might be a good way to make sure that you are getting essential nutrients. Keep in mind that vitamin/mineral supplements contain no calories and, without food, will do you little good. If you choose to supplement, look for brands that contain at least twenty vitamins and minerals. Each vitamin and mineral should supply no more than 150 percent of the recommended daily intake.

In general, take your supplement with a meal. Calcium is an exception. Calcium supplements should be taken as individual supplements and should be taken between meals.

Vegetarian Teen Meals and Meal Makeovers

The following are real stories about teens and the foods that they eat on a typical day. Using what they told us, we constructed typical vegetarian meals for a day representing a vegan diet, a lacto-ovo diet, a lacto-diet, and a raw-food diet. We'll show you how their diets stack up to nutritional needs and do a "diet makeover" for each vegetarian teen.

Beth's Typical Day as a Lacto-ovo Vegetarian

	CALORIES	PROTIEN (grams)	FAT (grams)	CALCIUM (mg)	IRON (mg)	VITAMIN B$_{12}$ (mcg)
Scrambled eggs (2)	202	14	14	86	1.4	1
Toast (2 pieces)	160	4	2	64	1.8	0
Margarine (2 tsps)	66	0	6	2	0	0
Milk (1 cup of 2% milk)	121	8	5	297	0.1	0.9
Grilled Cheese sandwich	428	19	24	414	2.1	0.4
Apple	73	0	0	5	0.1	0
Baby Carrots (10)	40	1	1	20	1	0
Cheese Ravioli with tomato sauce	341	15	15	172	3.1	0.4
Tossed salad (romaine, 2 cups)	16	2	0	20	0.6	0
Garlic Bread (3 pieces)	483	15	30	0	10.8	0
Milk (1 cup of 2% milk)	121	8	5	297	0.1	0.9
Salad dressing (French, 2 Tbsp)	134	1	12	4	0.2	0
Grapes (1 cup, red)	114	1	1	18	0.4	0
Ice Cream (1 cup, chocolate)	284	6	14	144	1.2	0.4
Totals	**2583**	**94**	**129**	**1543**	**22.9**	**4**
Recommended Intake (15 year old female)	**2200**	**44**	**(<30%kcal)**	**1300**	**15**	**2.4**

Beth is fifteen and has been a lacto-ovo vegetarian for two years. Her family is very supportive. They keep foods in the house that Beth can eat and plan family menus with vegetarian options for her. Beth is very active. She's on the school soccer team in the fall and plays basketball in the winter and spring. She is comfortable in the kitchen and often makes herself scrambled eggs before she goes to school.

At school she finds lots of options on the grill line (such as grilled cheese sandwiches) and usually picks up a piece of fresh fruit and some veggies on the à la carte line. She tries not to snack after school (she just drinks plenty of water at soccer or basketball practice) and comes home to a dinner that she usually eats with her family.

After doing her homework, she catches her favorite reality show on television and often has a snack. Below you'll find what Beth eats on a typical day and the amount of calories, protein, fat, calcium, iron, and B_{12} she consumes. The dietary recommendations for her age and sex are at the end.

So, how does Beth "stack up" to nutrient recommendations? Beth is doing a great job of getting the recommended amounts of protein, calcium, iron, and vitamin B_{12}. Her calorie intake is within a healthy range, especially since she is physically active. We can't really say if she is eating too many or not enough calories unless we keep track of her weight. If she has finished growing and is gaining weight on the calories that she is consuming, she is eating too many calories for her level of activity. If she is at a healthy weight and it is stable, then she is eating just the right amount.

BETH'S MENU MAKEOVER

Though Beth does well, she does need some makeover help. We started her diet makeover by looking at the amount of fat she is eating—about 130 grams of fat daily. That means she is getting about 45 percent of her calories from fat—too many. The maximum recommended intake is no more than 30 percent.

Beth's Menu Makeover

	CALORIES	PROTIEN (grams)	FAT (grams)	CALCIUM (mg)	IRON (mg)	VITAMIN B$_{12}$ (mcg)
Scrambled eggs (2)	202	14	14	86	1.4	1
Toast (2 pieces)	160	4	2	64	1.8	0
Margarine (2 tsps)	66	0	6	2	0	0
Milk (1 cup of skim milk)	86	8	0	302	0.1	0.9
Orange (1 fresh)	62	1	0	52	0.1	0
Grilled Cheese sandwich	428	19	24	414	2.1	0.4
Apple	73	0	0	5	0.1	0
Baby Carrots (10)	40	1	1	20	1	0
Raisins (½ cup)	248	2.5	0.5	40	1.7	0
Cheese Ravioli with tomato sauce	341	15	15	172	3.1	10.4
Tossed salad (romaine, 2 cups)	16	2	0	20	0.6	0
Garlic Bread (1 slice)	161	5	10	0	3.6	0
Milk (1 cup of skim milk)	86	8	0	302	0.1	0.9
Salad Dressing (French, 2 tbsp)	134	1	12	4	0.2	0
Steamed Broccoli (1 cup)	44	5	1	75	1.4	0
Grapes (1 cup red)	114	1	1	18	0.4	0
Fat-free frozen yogurt (1 cup chocolate)	207	11	2	326	1.7	1
Totals	**2468**	**97.5**	**88.5**	**1902**	**19.4**	**4.6**

The easiest things that she could do to reduce her fat intake are to:

- switch from 2% milk to skim milk.

- switch from regular ice cream to fat-free frozen yogurt.

- cut back on the garlic bread at dinner from three pieces to one piece.

If we compare her diet to the Food Guide Pyramid, we see that she is a little low on fruits and veggies, so she might add:

- An orange with breakfast.

- Raisins for an after-school snack (she can pop a box of raisins in her gym bag).

- A steamed vegetable at dinner.

After her makeover, her calories have stayed about the same, her protein, calcium, iron, and B_{12} are still within recommended levels, and she is now getting only 32 percent of her energy from fat. She still has a little way to go to reduce her fat intake, plus she is getting more saturated fats (fats primarily from animal products) than recommended.

Beth could think about a whole-grain cereal with fat-free yogurt and fruit as another breakfast option. She could also explore some other veggie options at school, such as a veggie burger or the salad bar. At home she could try some new recipes to boost her fruit and veggie intake. This vegan coleslaw recipe is full of vitamin C and fiber.

COLESLAW

This recipe is from RAW—The Uncook Book *by Julian Brotman and Erika Lenkert*

Servings: 2

    2 cups cabbage, shredded
    1 large cucumber, unpeeled, diced
    1 large carrot, shredded
    ¼ cup shredded onion
    1½ tablespoons cumin seed
    1½ teaspoons ground cumin
    3½ tablespoons fresh lemon juice
    ½ cup diced tomato
    1 teaspoon salt
    ⅓ cup olive oil

1 tablespoon minced garlic

Combine the above ingredients in a serving bowl. Mix and serve.

Nutritional Analysis Per Serving

Calories: 428

Fat: 38 grams (75.7 percent calories from fat)

Protein: 5 grams

Carbohydrate: 23 grams

Dietary fiber: 6 grams

Cholesterol: 0

Sodium: 1,113 milligramsetary

SAM: THE NEW VEGAN

Sam, a freshman in high school, decided to become a vegan after seeing a documentary about animal rights. After seeing how animals are treated when they are being raised to be food for humans, he decided right there and then: "No more meat or animal products for me—*ever*." His folks are hoping that it is a phase that will pass. They are not giving him a hard time about his decision, but they aren't doing much to help, either.

Sam started by cutting out all meat and animal products from his diet. His mom was worried about his calcium intake, so she insisted that he drink calcium-fortified soy milk. She's tried to be more adventurous in cooking and sometimes has tried some meatless, bean-based dishes such as vegan chili. She adds ground beef to the chili for the rest of the family after Sam dishes out what he wants.

Sam likes to sleep late, so he just has time for cold cereal before going off to school. At lunch he isn't sure what to eat as a new vegan, so he packs a peanut butter and jelly sandwich and then grabs chips, candy, and a soda to fill up. For dinner he just does the best he can to eat around what his mom puts out for the rest of the family. If he is still hungry before he goes to bed, he eats more cereal.

Sam's Typical Day as a Vegan

	CALORIES	PROTIEN (grams)	FAT (grams)	CALCIUM (mg)	IRON (mg)	VITAMIN B_{12} (mcg)
Capn' Crunch cereal (2 cups)	294	4	4	14	12.4	0
Soy Milk (1 cup)	80	8	2	10	1.4	0
Peanut butter and jelly sandwich (1)	351	12	15	60	2.3	0
Potato chips (2 oz bag)	304	4	20	14	0.9	0
Reese's Pieces (1 bag)	229	5.7	11.4	32	0.2	0
Vegan Chili (2 cups)	564	76	8	214	17.6	0
Hard Roll (1)	167	6	2	54	1.9	0
Margarine (1 tsp)	33	0	3	1	0	0
Coke (1 can)	153	0	0	11.1	0.1	0
Capn' Crunch cereal (2 cups)	294	4	4	14	2.4	0
Totals	**2469**	**120**	**69.4**	**424**	**49.2**	**0**
Recommended Intake (13 year old male)	**2500**	**45**	**(<30%kcal)**	**1300**	**8**	**1.8**

This daily chart shows that Sam is eating enough calories to maintain his weight and his intake of protein and fat is fine. In fact, he is only getting about 25 percent of his calories from fat—that's great. However, he is not getting enough calcium or B_{12} and is eating a lot of sugar. Comparing his intake to the Vegetarian Food Guide Pyramid shows that his diet is really in bad shape! He's eating no fruits, and the only vegetables he eats are the tomatoes in his vegan chili. The grains he is getting are mostly sweetened cereals packed with sugar and not the whole grains he should be eating.

SAM'S MENU MAKEOVER

Our goal for Sam's makeover was to get some more fruits and veggies in his diet, increase his intake of calcium and vitamin B_{12}, and replace some of the sugar with more healthful whole-grain products. By getting him to switch from his morning Capn' Crunch to a highly fortified whole-grain cereal, we were able to boost his calcium and vitamin B_{12} intake substantially. We also added a banana to breakfast (which he can eat on the bus on the way to school) and helped him figure out a way to pack not only a pb&j sandwich for lunch but also a can of V-8 juice. From the vending machine in school he can get an apple and pretzels.

Sam's Menu Makeover

	CALORIES	PROTIEN (grams)	FAT (grams)	CALCIUM (mg)	IRON (mg)	VITAMIN B_{12} (mcg)
Total Cereal (1.5 cups)	158	4.5	1.5	387	27	11.5
Soy Milk (1 cup)	80	8	2	10	1.4	0
Banana (1 medium)	108	1	1	7	0.4	0
Peanut butter and jelly sandwich (1)	351	12	15	60	2.3	0
Pretzels (10)	229	5	2	22	2.6	0
V-8 juice, 12-oz can	69	3	0	41	1.5	0
Apple (1 medium)	73	0	0	5	0.1	0
Vegan Chili (2 cups)	564	76	8	214	17.6	0
Hard Roll (1)	167	6	2	54	1.9	0
Margarine (1 tsp)	33	0	3	1	0	0
Spinach salad with tomato (2 cups)	52	4	1	69	2.4	0
Salad Dressing (2 tbsp)	144	0	18	0	0	0
Broccoli 1(cup steamed)	44	4	0	72	1.4	0
Soy milk (1cup)	80	8	2	10	1.4	0
Capn' Crunch Cereal (1 cup)	147	2	2	7	6.2	0
Raisins (¼ cup)	124	1.3	0	20	0.8	0
Totals	**2299**	**134**	**57.5**	**959**	**66.2**	**11.5**

His mom's vegan chili is full of healthy legumes and beans and is providing great protein. We suggest that she make it up in larger quantities and freeze it for Sam so he can zap some in the microwave on the nights that the family is eating a meat-based dinner. We suggest a salad (Sam likes spinach and tomatoes) and a cooked veggie (broccoli is good because it has some calcium and other important nutrients). Since he *loves* Capn' Crunch, we kept that for a bedtime snack but we cut the quantity in half and added some soy milk and some raisins.

After his makeover, he is now getting the food groups recommended on the Vegetarian Food Guide Pyramid, enough iron and B_{12} and 23 percent of his calories from fat. His calcium is still a little low, so his next step might be to ask his mom to buy soy milk fortified with calcium or replace all of his sugar-sweetened cereal with a calcium-fortified cereal. He could also try orange juice fortified with calcium. It would be good for Sam to start to try some alternative protein sources. We've included this very simple recipe for Sloppy Joes made with textured soy protein that he could try the next time his mom lets him in the kitchen!

SLOPPY JOES

This recipe is courtesy of the Indiana Soybean Board, www.soyfoods.com/index.html

Servings: 4
- 1 cup textured soy protein (TSP, also called TVP)
- 1 cup boiling water
- 1 16-ounce can sloppy joe sauce
- 4 whole-wheat hamburger rolls

To rehydrate the TVP, place it in a medium saucepan and pour the boiling water over it. Add the sloppy joe sauce to the TVP. Cook over low heat until heated through. To serve, pour the TVP mixture over the hamburger rolls.

Nutritional Analysis Per Serving
Calories: 399
Fat: 3 grams (7 percent calories from fat)
Protein: 47 grams
Carbohydrates: 52 grams
Dietary fiber: 16 grams
Cholesterol: 0
Sodium: 946 milligrams

Sue is fourteen and has been a vegetarian since she was twelve. In just the last year, she decided to go vegan. Her family is not at all supportive. They think that she is calling herself a vegetarian to disguise an eating disorder or that she is just trying to get attention by making mealtime difficult for everyone. For the moment her family has given up on making a big deal about what she does, or doesn't, eat. They are hoping that this is just a phase that she is going through.

Sue is on her own in the kitchen and likes to cook, but she is so busy with school that she doesn't have much time to plan her diet. Her "typical menu" shows it, too! On this typical day, she consumed fewer than 700 calories while the recommended intake for a girl her age is about 2,200 calories. She is not getting enough protein, calcium, iron, or B_{12} either. She hasn't hit the mark for any of the food groups. If Sue continues to eat like this, she could run into some significant health problems.

Sue's Typical Day as a Vegan

	CALORIES	PROTIEN (grams)	FAT (grams)	CALCIUM (mg)	IRON (mg)	VITAMIN B_{12} (mcg)
Toast (1 piece)	69	3	1	20	0.9	0
Cold rice-and-veggie salad (1 cup)	189	4	4	35	1	0
Apple (1 medium)	73	0	0	5	0.1	0
Tofu tacos	280	17	11	121	2	0
Soy Milk (1 cup)	80	8	2	10	1.4	0
Total	**691**	**32**	**18**	**191**	**5.4**	**0**
Recommended Intake (14 year-old female)	**2000**	**46**	**<30%kcal**	**1300**	**15**	**2.4**

For her menu makeover, the first thing Sue needs to do is to start eating more. She is at a critical stage of growth, and her body needs calories, protein, and calcium to build bone, muscle, and organ tissue. If she is not eating because of some emotional distress, anxiety, or depression, she needs to talk to a supportive adult and get some help. Depression and anxiety are treatable illnesses.

Sue's Menu Makeover

	CALORIES	PROTIEN (grams)	FAT (grams)	CALCIUM (mg)	IRON (mg)	VITAMIN B$_{12}$ (mcg)
Toast (1 piece)	69	3	1	20	0.9	0
Peanut Butter (1 tbsp)	93	4	8	8	0.4	0
Orange Juice (calcium fortified, ½ cup)	55	1	0	150	0.4	0
Cold rice-and-veggie salad (1cup)	189	4	4	35	1	0
Apple (1 medium)	73	0	0	5	0.1	0
Tofu yogurt (1 cup)	254	9	5	309	2.8	0
Dried apricots (10 pieces)	80	3	0	20	2	0
Tofu Tacos	280	17	11	121	2	0
Soy Milk (VitaSoy, 1 cup)	190	7	6	80	0.7	0
Green Salad: Romaine lettuce (1cup)	8	1	0	20	0.6	0
Pepper Slices (½ pepper)	25	1	0	10	0.5	0
Cherry tomatoes (5)	20	0	0	5	0.5	0
Salad Dressing (French, low-cal, 2 tbsp)	44	0	16	4	0.2	0
Toast (1 piece)	69	3	1	20	0.09	0
Peanut Butter (1 tbsp)	93	4	8	8	0.4	0
Sub Total	**1283**	**48**	**35**	**748**	**10.3**	**0**
Second Step:						
Vegetable Soup (1 cup)	122	4	4	22	1.1	0
Whole-grain bread (2 pieces)	138	6	2	40	1.8	0
Peanut butter (1 tbsp)	94	4	8	6.5	0.3	0
Doritos chips (1 cup)	129	2	7	38	0.4	0
Salsa (½ cup)	35	1.5	0.5	36	1.3	0
Totals	**1801**	**65.5**	**56.5**	**890.5**	**15.2**	**0**

We started Sue's makeover by adding some protein and fruit at breakfast. A little peanut butter on toast and a small glass of juice doesn't add any time to her breakfast preparation and does add some important protein at the beginning of her day, which will help her concentrate in morning classes.

For lunch we suggest adding a tofu or soy yogurt and some dried fruit. For dinner, the addition of a green salad and a switch from regular soy milk to a fortified soy milk would give her a big nutrient boost. If she can eat some peanut butter on toast before she goes to bed, she will boost her protein intake and get another grain serving. If the toast is whole grain, that will be even better.

Makeovers, and changing the way we eat, often go in steps. Even after our makeover, Sue is not meeting the recommended amounts of calories, calcium, iron, and B_{12}, but she has made significant improvements in her diet. As a second step in the makeover, we have suggested some "extras" that will help her diet even more. With a multivitamin supplement, she can boost her calcium, iron, and B_{12} to recommended levels and can help cover other nutrients in which she may be deficient. She needs to continue to work on getting enough fruits and veggies in her diet and to experiment in the kitchen with vegan dishes. We've included a simple recipe for Tempeh Chili that she might try the next time she feels adventurous.

TEMPEH CHILI

This recipe is courtesy of the Indiana Soybean Board, www.soyfoods.com/index.html

Servings: 4

- 8 ounces tempeh
- 2 tablespoons oil
- 1 large onion, diced
- 2½ cups tomato sauce
- 3 tablespoons chili powder (or to taste)
- 1 tablespoon tamari
- 1 tablespoon dry mustard
- 2 teaspoons garlic powder
- 1 teaspoon ground cumin

Cut the tempeh into small cubes. Sauté the tempeh in the oil for about 10 minutes, until lightly browned. Add the remaining ingredients and simmer for 20 minutes.

Nutritional Analysis Per Serving (excluding unknown items)
Calories: 261
Fat: 13 grams (45 percent calories from fat)
Protein: 15 grams
Carbohydrates: 28 grams
Fiber: 59 grams
Cholesterol: 28 grams
Sodium: 1,240 milligrams

AMY: A LACTO-VEGETARIAN

Amy is an eighteen-year-old lacto-vegetarian and a freshman at a community college. She lives in an apartment with two girlfriends from high school. They love living on their own and being able to choose when and what they eat. Amy tries to get a good breakfast, but lunch is usually on the run between classes. The roommates try to make a point of eating their evening meal together so that they can catch up with each other and hear how classes (and romances!) are going.

Nutrient-wise, Amy's diet doesn't look too bad. Her weight is fairly stable, so her calorie intake is good. She is getting enough protein and about 31 percent of her calories from total fat. Her calcium, iron, and B_{12} are a little low, but not too bad. When we look at her diet from the Vegetarian Food Guide Pyramid viewpoint, we see some areas to work on. She isn't getting enough servings from any food groups except from the one labeled "Other." A substantial number of her calories—about 50 percent—are coming from junk food, including chips, snack crackers, soft drinks, and cookies. Also, since she left high school, her physical activity has decreased. Amy needs a menu makeover before her junk food habits and decreased physical activity lead to weight gain. We also need to help her eat more nutrient-dense foods.

Amy's Typical Day as a Lacto-Vegetarian

	CALORIES	PROTIEN (grams)	FAT (grams)	CALCIUM (mg)	IRON (mg)	VITAMIN B_{12} (mcg)
Crispy Wheat and Raisin cereal (1 cup)	153	3	1	27	0.2	0
2 % Milk (1 cup)	121	8	5	297	0.1	0.9
Orange Juice (1 cup)	110	2	1	25	0.4	0
Power Bar	230	10	2	350	5.4	0.1
Chips (2 oz bag)	304	4	20	14	0.9	0
Cheezits (30 crackers)	150	3	9	45	1.5	0
Soft Drink (12-oz can)	153	0	0	11	0.1	0
Salad						
Lettuce (2 cups)	16	2	0	20	0.6	0
Sprouts (½ cup)	15	1.5	0	6.7	0.5	0
Tomato (2 slices)	8	0	0	2	0.2	0
Cheese, shredded (cheddar; ¼ cup)	113	7	9	204	0.2	0.3
Garbanzo beans (½ cup)	134	7	2	40	2.3	0
Oreos (6 cookies)	320	4	14	0	1.4	0
Totals	**1827**	**51.5**	**63**	**1042**	**13.8**	**1.3**
Recommended Intake (18 year-old female)	**2200**	**44**	**<30%kcal**	**1300**	**15**	**2.4**

We didn't change much about her breakfast except switch her milk to skim milk and suggest an orange instead of orange juice to increase her fiber intake and control her appetite. What she eats and drinks on campus needs some work, however. The Power Bar is a good snack to eat on the run. Unlike many snacks, it is fairly high in protein and contains calcium, iron, and B_{12}. We replaced many of the empty calories she eats while on campus with more nutrient-dense calories. Instead of grabbing chips and crackers between classes, she is able to buy a veggie wrap, a yogurt, and a diet soft drink at a coffee shop on campus.

Amy's Menu Makeover

	CALORIES	PROTIEN (grams)	FAT (grams)	CALCIUM (mg)	IRON (mg)	VITAMIN B$_{12}$ (mcg)
Crispy Wheat and Raisin cereal (1 cup)	153	3	1	27	0.2	0
Fat-free milk (1 cup)	86	8	0	302	0.1	0.9
Fresh orange	62	1	0	52	0.1	0
Power Bar (1)	230	10	2	350	5.4	0.1
Veggie-wrap sandwich	250	9	4	150	3	0.3
Fat-free yogurt (1 cup)	122	11	0	370	0.6	1.1
Diet soft drink	0	0	0	0	0	0
Salad						
Lettuce (2 cups)	16	2	0	20	0.6	0
Sprouts (½ cup)	15	1.5	0	6.7	0.5	0
Tomato (2 slices)	8	0	0	2	0.2	0
Cheese, shredded (cheddar; ¼ cup)	113	7	9	204	0.2	0.3
Garbanzo beans (½ cup)	134	7	2	40	2.3	0
Whole wheat roll	75	2	1	30	0.7	0
Salad dressing (2 tbsp reduced-fat)	32	0	2	2.8	0	0
Margarine (1 tsp)	33	0	3	1	0	0
Banana (1 medium)	108	1	1	7	0.4	0
Whole wheat crackers (6 crackers)	106	2	4	12	0.8	0
Oreos (3)	160	2	7	0	0.7	0
Totals	**1543**	**64.5**	**29**	**1577**	**15.1**	**2.7**

Her dinner salad is a great idea, and we've only added a whole wheat roll and some margarine to that meal to help her feel more satisfied. She gets hungry when she studies late, so we've added a banana and some low-fat crackers. We kept her beloved Oreos but reduced her usual intake by half. Ideally, she should try to wean herself off of them.

Now that she lives on her own, she may want to start to find some quick and easy recipes that she could make ahead for dinner. We've included one of our family favorites—Broccoli Mostaccoli Bake—that uses skim milk, lower-fat cheese, and frozen broccoli. (Mostaccoli is tubular-shaped pasta, but if you can't find it in your grocery store, you can substitute penne pasta.) We also recommended that Amy find some regular physical activity that she enjoys doing. Regular physical activity will not only help her control her weight as she heads to adulthood, it will also help her handle the stress of college and help her sleep better.

MOSTACCIOLI BROCCOLI BAKE

This recipe is an old favorite in Leslie's house.

Servings: 4
- 1 quart water
- ½ teaspoon salt
- 1 cup mostaccioli (or penne)
- 1 tablespoon margarine
- 1 tablespoon flour
- ⅔ cup skim milk
- ¼ cup grated Parmesan cheese
- ¼ teaspoon salt
- ½ clove garlic, minced
- ⅛ teaspoon dried thyme
- ⅛ teaspoon ground nutmeg
- 10 ounces frozen broccoli, cooked, drained, and chopped
- ¼ cup shredded Swiss cheese

Pre-heat the oven to 375˚ F.

Boil the water with ½ teaspoon salt in a large deep pot. Add the mostaccioli; stir to separate. Cook, uncovered, after the water returns to a full rolling boil, for 11 to 12 minutes. Stir occasionally. Drain and rinse under hot water.

In a medium saucepan, melt the margarine. Stir in the flour until well blended. Add the milk all at once. Cook until thickened, stirring constantly. Stir in the Parmesan cheese, remaining ¼ teaspoon salt, garlic, thyme, and nutmeg.

Remove from the heat.

In a medium bowl, combine the cooked mostaccioli, cheese sauce, and broccoli. Turn the mixture into 5 x 8-inch pan. Sprinkle the Swiss cheese over the top.

Bake for 10 or 15 minutes, or until heated through.

Nutritional Analysis Per Serving

Calories:188

Fat: 7 grams (33 percent calories from fat)

Protein: 10 grams

Carbohydrates: 22 grams

Dietary fiber: 2 grams

Cholesterol: 11 milligrams

Sodium: 586 milligrams

DEREK: THE RAW FOODIST

Derek has been a vegan for about three years. On a recent trip to San Francisco, his aunt took him to a really cool raw-food restaurant. Nothing was cooked and the menu was full of foods and flavors and colors that he had never seen in foods before! He had a pizza (the crust was made of buckwheat sprouts) and a fruit smoothie. He felt so light and energized after the meal that he decided to take his veganism one step further: He wanted to become a raw foodist.

Derek had a hard time identifying raw foods beyond fruits and veggies, and it shows. He started by eating a lot of fruits, vegetables, and salads. He was hungry much of the time, and he was eating the same foods over and over again. His typical menu shows that he wasn't getting enough calories, protein, calcium, or vitamin B_{12}. His fat intake is in the healthy range, at about 25 percent of calories, but he isn't eating many calories to begin with, so there isn't enough fat in his diet to help him feel full. He is getting his iron mostly from spinach, which is not bioavailable, so he needs additional sources. While he knows that he needs to get some source of B_{12}, he stopped eating fortified cereal because he knows it is not considered a "raw food." He just hasn't figured out what to do about that yet! Derek needs to start by learning a lot more about being a raw foodist and how to prepare a variety of foods that will help keep him healthy.

Derek's Typical Day as a Raw Foodist

	CALORIES	PROTIEN (grams)	FAT (grams)	CALCIUM (mg)	IRON (mg)	VITAMIN B$_{12}$ (mcg)
Orange (1 medium)	62	1	0	52	0.1	0
Apple (1 medium)	73	0	0	5	0.1	0
Walnuts (¼ cup)	164	4	16	26	0.7	0
Salad greens (Spinach, 2 cups)	14	2	2	60	1.6	0
Sprouts (1 cup)	30	3	0	13.4	1	0
Red pepper slices (1 cup)	40	1	0	13	0.7	0
Lemon juice (2 tbsp)	6	0	0	3	0	0
Apple	73	0	0	5	0.1	0
Raisins (¼ cup)	124	1.3	0	20	0.8	0
Greens, loose-leaf 1 cup	10	1	0	38	0.8	0
Banana	108	1	1	7	0.4	0
Sprouts (1 cup)	30	3	0	13.4	1	0
Almonds 2 (tbsp)	76	3	7	28	0.5	0
Mushrooms (1 cup raw)	18	2	0	4	0.8	0
Raisins (¼ cup)	124	1.3	0	20	0.8	0
Total	**952**	**23.6**	**26**	**308**	**9.4**	**0**
Recommended Intake (17 year old male)	**3000**	**59**	**<30%kcal**	**1300**	**11**	**2.4**

Raw foodists are vegans who believe that raw cuisine is "living food"—that is, foods that are still alive. These include fruits, vegetables, grains, beans, nuts, roots, and seeds. In addition, they believe that temperatures greater than 120˚ F destroy the enzymes in foods and make them less nourishing. That means that any food that is processed or baked (including bottled salad dressing, heat-processed oils, breads, and cereals, and heat-processed soy-bean products like tofu) are off limits to a raw foodist. The primary ways that foods are processed for a raw foodist include: dehydration that involves drying foods at low temperatures (about 100° F), pureeing, chopping, blending, and juicing. Beans, grains, and seeds are sprouted and soaked.

In his makeover Derek's protein is going to come primarily from nuts, sprouted beans, seeds, grains, and vegetables. His fat will come from nuts, seeds, grains, and fat-containing fruits and vegetables (olives and avocados), and he'll get his vitamins and minerals through these sources as well. Excessive intakes of some foods (such as raw spinach or sprouted-wheat products) may interfere with his body's ability to absorb some vitamins and minerals.

Derek's Menu Makeover

	CALORIES	PROTIEN (grams)	FAT (grams)	CALCIUM (mg)	IRON (mg)	VITAMIN B$_{12}$ (mcg)
Orange (1 medium)	62	1	0	52	0.1	0
Apple (1 medium)	73	0	0	5	0.1	0
Walnuts (¼ cup)	164	4	16	26	0.7	0
Salad greens (Spinach, 2 cups)	14	2	2	60	1.6	0
Sprouts (1 cup)	30	3	0	13.4	1	0
Red pepper slices (1 cup)	40	1	0	13	0.7	0
Lemon juice (2 tbsp)	6	0	0	3	0	0
Apple	73	0	0	5	0.1	0
Flaxseed crackers (2 crackers:						
see recipe on page xxx)	306	12	20	136	4	0
Pumpkin seed "cheese" (½ cup; see recipe on page 178)	286	6	11	46	2	0
Raisins (¼ cup)	124	1.3	0	20	0.8	0
Greens, loose-leaf 1 cup	10	1	0	38	0.8	0
Banana	108	1	1	7	0.4	0
Sprouts (1 cup)	30	3	0	13.4	1	0
Almonds 2 (tbsp)	76	3	7	28	0.5	0
Mushrooms (1 cup raw)	18	2	0	4	0.8	0
Garlic Bread (1 slice)	358	9	29	74	2	0
Total	**1902**	**50.6**	**86**	**563.8**	**17.4**	**0**

For Derek's makeover, we worked in some recipes from a raw cookbook (*RAW, the Uncook Book*, by Juliana with Erika Lenkert.)

We chose foods that would help replace breads in his diet—flaxseed crackers and garlic bread made from walnuts, flaxseeds, and jícama—and some pumpkin seed "cheese" for a creamy spread on the crackers. He'll need to learn how to increase the variety in his diet by spending some time experimenting in the kitchen; otherwise, he will quickly tire of a raw-food diet and will also be risking his nutritional well-being.

With the addition of these foods (the recipes can be found in the following pages), his calories have more than doubled and his protein intake meets his requirements. His fat intake has increased to about 40 percent of the calories in his diet, which is a little high. If he simply eats more fruits and veggies, he will boost his calorie intake and reduce his calories from fat down to recommended levels. While he has increased his calcium intake, it is still not enough to meet recommended levels, and he still has no vitamin B_{12} in his diet. He needs a vitamin B_{12} source, so adding a multivitamin/mineral supplement to his diet and a calcium supplement (taken between meals) is probably a good idea.

FLAXSEED CRACKERS

Servings: 12 crackers
⅛ cup chopped red bell pepper
⅛ cup chopped cilantro
⅔ cup sun-dried tomatoes
1 ¼ cups diced fresh tomatoes
1 teaspoon minced jalapeno pepper
1 tablespoon minced fresh garlic
1 tablespoon olive oil
1 teaspoon salt
2 cups flaxseeds

Place the bell pepper, cilantro, sun-dried tomatoes, fresh tomatoes, jalapeño, garlic, olive oil, and salt in a food processor and purée. Transfer the contents to a large bowl and mix in the flaxseeds. Pour the flaxseed mixture onto an oiled solid dehydrator sheet (approximately 12 x 16 inches). Dehydrate at 90˚ F. for 4 hours or until the mixture is dry. Cut into 4-inch squares and transfer the crackers onto a mesh dehydrating rack. Dehydrate on mesh until the crackers are crisp, about 5 hours.

Nutritional Analysis Per Cracker
Calories: 145
Fat: 10 grams (62 percent calories from fat)
Protein: 5 grams
Carbohydrates: 11 grams
Dietary fiber: 8 grams
Cholesterol: 0
Sodium: 190 milligrams

PUMPKIN SEED "CHEESE"

Servings: Nine ¼-cup servings
    2 cups pumpkin seeds, roasted
    1 bunch fresh parsley
    1 tablespoon garlic
    1 tablespoon minced fresh ginger
    1 teaspoon minced jalapeño
    1½ teaspoons salt
    ⅓ cup olive oil
    ½ cup fresh lemon juice

In a large container, soak the pumpkin seeds with enough water to cover for at least 15 minutes. Place the seeds in a mesh sieve to drain. Put the seeds in a food processor with remaining ingredients. Blend until creamy.
Will keeps in the refrigerator for 2 days.

Nutritional Analysis Per Cup

Calories: 143

Fat: 11 grams (69 percent calories from fat)

Protein: 2 grams

Carbohydrate: 10 grams

Dietary Fiber: 2 grams

Cholesterol: 0

Sodium: 362 milligrams

GARLIC "BREAD"

Servings: 8 slices

1 jícama

1 cup walnuts and/or almonds

1 cup flaxseeds

1½ teaspoons sea salt

½ cup olive oil

¼ cup diced red bell pepper

½ cup minced garlic

½ cup fresh lemon juice

Slice the jícama into eight slices (they should be as thin as possible) and spread in a single layer on a solid dehydrator sheet.

Grind the flaxseeds and walnuts and/or almonds very fine until they are the consistency of powder. Put in a bowl and add the remaining ingredients. Mix thoroughly. Drizzle the mixture over the jícama.

Dehydrate in a dehydrator at 100˚ F for 8 hours, or until chewy.

Nutritional Analysis Per Slice

Calories: 358

Fat: 29 grams (73 percent calories from fat)

Protein: 9 grams

Carbohydrate: 20 grams

Dietary Fiber: 11 grams

Cholesterol: 0

Sodium: 364 milligrams

If you want to do your own menu makeover, record everything that you eat or drink on a typical day. Or better yet, record everything that you eat for three or four days. Enter your intake in a nutrient composition software package or online resource. (See page 000 for information on diet-analysis websites.)

If your analysis is for more than one day, average it out to a one-day level. Compare the one-day average of servings to recommended numbers of servings of different food groups, such as fruits, vegetables, and grains in the Vegetarian Food Guide Pyramid. Start adding (or eliminating) foods until your nutrient intake starts to get closer to recommended levels. Start with easy changes and continue to work on your diet over a few weeks or months until you've found foods and eating patterns that meet recommended levels, keep you healthy, and that you enjoy eating!

Summing It Up

- Vegetarian teens should take special care to get enough calories, protein, fat, calcium, iron, and vitamin B_{12} in their diets. Use the Vegetarian Food Guide to find the number of servings of particular foods that are needed each day.

- There are ways to modify your diet to meet dietary requirements and remain a vegetarian, whether you are an ovo-lacto, vegan, or raw foodist.

- Vegetarian teens should assess their own typical diets and plan their own makeovers as needed for their current and future health.

Conclusion

It is our hope that this book will serve as both a reference manual and a source of inspiration for vegetarian teenagers. It may sometimes feel as though you're fighting an uphill battle against a powerful, consumerist, meat-eating society, but rest assured that you are a positive part of the future. Your efforts will not go unnoticed or unappreciated. Vegetarianism is increasingly popular in the United States. People of many different ages, socio-economic backgrounds, and cultures are becoming aware of the negative repercussions of this country's voracious appetite for meat. Animals are being mistreated; they are bred distinctly for consumption and cruelly slaughtered after short, unhappy lives. The environment is suffering as a result of the many resources exploited to produce food for a world full of carnivores. Other social issues, like poverty and world hunger, also play a role in the decision to "go veg." Many vegetarians recognize that more people can be fed with grain products than with meat. Further, the extreme size and scope of the meat industry makes it difficult to regulate. Products contaminated with salmonella, or even mad cow disease in some countries, are being sold in supermarkets and served in school lunch lines. This industry is so powerful that they can control the media's messages about meat. Misconceptions such as the need for protein only found in meat, or the masculinity inherent in consuming steaks, is propagated. These messages about the importance of meat in the diet have contributed to the high incidence of heart disease, stroke, cancer, diabetes, and obesity in the United States.

When you choose vegetarianism, you are making a conscious decision to improve your health. A diet based on plant foods such as whole grains, beans, and fruits and vegetables is an investment in your own health and future as well as the health and future of the world around you. You will most likely experience lower cholesterol, lower blood pressure, and a healthy weight. You may also experience a better sense of well-being, overall health, and/or the feeling of living more in tune with nature.

Perhaps the power you gain over your own health will spark a desire to fight for social change. Often when you choose to differentiate yourself with new diet choices, you gain the confidence to stand up for other causes. Vegetarian teenagers all over the country are organizing and protesting for animal rights. They are also fighting for civil rights and environmental issues. Visit local coffee shops or college campuses to find out how to get involved. If you live in a small town, you may have to be a pioneer. However you choose to get involved, whether on an individual, community, or worldwide level, know that you are an integral part of the future. You *do* have the power to raise awareness about these important issues and to make change.

Whenever you feel isolated or frustrated by your decision to pursue a vegetarian lifestyle, remind yourself of the testimonials presented in *The Vegetarian Manifesto*. There are thousands of kids out there refusing to eat their grandmother's meat loaf. And thousands of kids who know that animals have feelings, too, and shouldn't be killed inhumanely. Your job as a young vegetarian is to be a shining example of the rewards your choices reap. You are in a powerful position to influence many people. Stand firmly behind your beliefs and speak with conviction when you are challenged by your parents or your peers. Use the resources mentioned in this book to keep up on the issues, and to maintain your healthy diet. Congratulations on making a lifestyle choice that will not only greatly benefit your health, but the health of the world around you.

REFERENCES USED IN THIS BOOK

American Journal of Clinical Nutrition, "The Fourth International Congress on Vegetarian Nutrition," Proceedings from a symposium held in Loma Linda, CA. September 2003, Volume 78, Number 3 (Supplement).

Davis, Brenda and Melina, Vesanto, *Becoming Vegan: The Complete Guide to Adopting a Healthy Plant-Based Diet.* Summertown: Book Publishing Company, 2000.

Hall, Dede, *The Starving Student's Vegetarian Cookbook.* New York: Warner, 2001.

Insel, Paul, Turner, R. Elaine and Ross, Don. *Discovering Nutrition.* Sudbury: Jones and Bartlett Publishers, 2003.

Krizmanic, Judy. *A Teen's Guide to Going Vegetarian.* New York: Puffin, 1994.

Marcus, Erik. *Vegan: The New Ethics of Eating.* Ithaca: McBooks Press, 2001.

Melina, Vesanto, Davis, Brenda and Harrison Victoria. *Becoming Vegetarian: The Complete Guide to Adopting a Healthy Vegetarian Diet.* Summertown: Book Publishing Company, 1995.

Null, Gary. *The Vegetarian Handbook.* New York: St. Martin's Griffin, 1996.

Schlosser, Eric. *Fast Food Nation: The Dark Side of the All-American Meal.* New York: Harper Collins, 2002.

Vegetarian Times. *Vegetarian Beginner's Guide. Everything You Need to Know to Be a Healthy Vegetarian.* New York: Wiley, 1996.

Acknowledgments

We'd like to thank the vegetarian teens for offering their stories so candidly and honestly. We'd also like to thank Emily Trenkner, Bonnie Manning, and Debora Yost for their help in the preparation and editing of the book. Teresa would like to thank her parents for supporting her as a vegetarian teen. Finally, Leslie and Cheryl would like to thank their husbands for their encouragement and support throughout the writing of the book.

The authors also gratefully acknowledge the "vegetarianteen.com" and "PETA.org" websites as sources of information for this book. We thank them for granting us permission to pose questions and access information for their sites.